BOCCONI
UNIVERSITY
PRESS

Fernando Napolitano

INFLUENCE, RELEVANCE AND GROWTH FOR A CHANGING WORLD

How to Survive & Thrive with IRG™ Beyond ESG

Foreword by **Stefano Caselli**
Afterword by **KC Sullivan**

Cover: Cristina Bernasconi, Milan
Typesetting: Alberto Bellanti, Milan

Copyright © 2023 Bocconi University Press
EGEA S.p.A.

EGEA S.p.A.
Via Salasco, 5 - 20136 Milano
Tel. 02/5836.5751 – Fax 02/5836.5753
egea.edizioni@unibocconi.it – www.egeaeditore.it

First edition: September 2023

ISBN Domestic Edition	979-12-80623-22-5
ISBN International Edition	978-88-31322-95-9
ISBN Digital Domestic Edition	978-88-238-8705-3
ISBN Digital International Edition	978-88-31322-96-6

Print: Logo s.r.l., Borgoricco (PD)

Table of Contents

Foreword

by *Stefano Caselli*

We are living in times that are simultaneously fascinating and complex. As a leading business school, our academic nature and mission as educators propel us to trace back to the forces shaping our social context, identifying emerging trends and new dimensions that need to be quantified, measured, and managed.

The world of business, as well as the context it operates in, is completely transformed. We face a series of formidable challenges brought about by the intensity of technological progress and societal changes. Artificial intelligence, cybersecurity, regenerative medicine, energy, migration, inequality are just a few of the hurdles we must collectively address to maintain balanced and inclusive economic growth.

Over the years, companies have shown a great capacity to capture and respond to the needs expressed by society, sometimes anticipating trends more nimbly than other entities such as the media and governmental and non-governmental organizations. They have adeptly addressed, with a better vision and perspective, the needs expressed by various actors, needs that only partially relate to profit.

In modern times, companies have been able to respond to a range of issues. Particularly in western economies, a trusted collaboration has been created between these significant corporations and citizens, with the former often acting as "problem solvers", supporting governments and other institutional actors in meeting the needs of the population.

This trust in large companies has prompted them to undertake increasingly significant roles, pushing them to embrace topics that range far beyond their specific industrial sector. Companies today promote policies on issues such as social security and the environment, demonstrating a positive synergy with governmental policies.

However, previously adopted Corporate Social Responsibility policies and the more recent ESG policies, while of vital importance, are not always capable of fully addressing the ever-new and changing challenges of our time. Faced with this situation, companies often take the initiative to adapt and directly respond to the real needs of both the market and the population at large.

It is therefore crucial to understand how companies can play a key role in this new social position, going beyond mere financial analysis of business results, creating a constructive dialogue with political institutions for shared and sustainable growth.

"Influence, Relevance and Growth (IRG) for a Changing World. How to Survive & Thrive beyond ESG World" and the author's proposed solution are timely and pragmatic. He represents a forecast in a post-sustainability world where ESG continues to play a pivotal role for transparency, accountability, and general awareness on the need to firmly tackle environmental challenges. The IRG incorporates and accounts for its successes.

The IRG metric thus allows measuring, through the analysis of 10 parameters, whether and how much a company is ready to confront and manage these new challenges or position itself as an intermediary subject, bridging existing gaps between the needs expressed by the population and the responses of political decision-makers. Companies, in fact, do not seek to replace politics, but propose themselves as useful partners to help the political scene be more responsive to the needs of citizens.

Today, issues such as the introduction of artificial intelligence, climate change-related issues, and the use of various energy sources, ethical issues related to regenerative medicine, and genetically modified food are being addressed. These are topics where the combined contribution of politics and businesses can make a difference.

The IRG indicators therefore represent the latest tool that allows companies to self-assess - and external stakeholders to evaluate - the capacity to respond to these issues.

IRG is based on 10 quantifiable parameters that, leveraging artificial intelligence, measure whether a company is ready or not to operate in this new environment, where critical skills must be transferred to other interested parties to regain balance over time. In this way, the possibility of a fruitful synergy between companies and political decision-makers to tackle the future challenges is enhanced.

Acknowledgements

My first debt of gratitude is to my former partners Reggie Van Lee, Mark Gerencser and Kris Kelly, from Booz Allen Hamilton, where I have been privileged to spent 20 years of my working life. The IRG system follows work co-authored with them. Rocco Sabelli was the first to suggest that I needed to write a book, setting me on this journey with the invaluable support of an Irish writer and others.

As I progressed, I benefited from the constructive critiques of thought leaders from my work of the last thirty years. My generous friend and former colleague Pietro Candela pioneered with me the early IRG architecture. Fulvio Conti and Francesco Starace helped illuminate the path through feedback that highlighted new dimensions. My conversations with Fedele Confalonieri and Paolo Scaroni contributed to appreciate world's affairs and human beings' behavior with more realism. It is encouraging to see leaders of diverse industries and professions share the same sense of urgency. Luigi Ferraris was a valued early advocate, and Giuseppe Castagna, Rocco Sabelli, Bill Mayer and Ron Spogli added global perspectives from finance, engineering pragmatism and multiculturalism. Anthony Viscusi's "red pencil" was the ultimate test for the content and the narrative. David Rhodes provided a precious media foresight.

Richard Vietor's irreproachable academic rigor helped me marshal the feedback from the professional and industrial experiences of Lucio Stanca, Stefano Sala, Martin Brannigan, Claudio Vaccarella, Suzanne Helm, Ryan O'Keeffee, Francesco Taranto, Salvo Arena, Gregorio Consoli, Filippo Modulo, Jeff Libshutz, Angelo De Tomasi, Agostino Carloni, Gina Nieri, Mike Nowlis, Marco Andreassi, Alessandro Fracassi, Corrado Passera, Libby Fidler, Haresh Patel, Tim Buchner, Francesco Cardinali, Luca Torchia, Matteo Cidda, Massimo Angelini, Ferdinando Pozzani, Jeffrey Hedberg, Egidio Pardini, Ketty Maisonrouge, Angelo Maria Petroni and Jules Goffre. I am grateful to all.

Special thanks to Stefano Caselli and KC Sullivan for their generosity in writing the preface and afterword. Gimede Gigante and Andrea Cerri for their academic advice.

I have been particularly privileged in my life to be surrounded since I can remember by such smart people. It was so since the outset in the form of my scientist father, the late Luigi Gerardo Napolitano, whose intellect so influenced me. None of this could have been achieved without the constant and enduring support and serenity of my immediate family members Matilde, Allegra, Anastasia and Luigi Gerardo, who challenge me in our frequent discussions. And Saigon, our dog, my companion as I distilled my thoughts on our long walks in Todi.

Bosses are under increasing pressure to take stances on social issues. How should they respond? … Anticipating changes to political and social norms is hard. But it is a vital part of the CEO's job description.

— *The Economist*, November 30, 2017

The United States government needs to do proper things … they need help.

— Jamie Dimon, CEO of JP Morgan Chase

A business leader today must do more than worry about profits… what they need to do is talk about how to increase the odds that conditions exist in which their businesses can operate successfully.

— Richard Haass, President Emeritus of the Council on Foreign Relations in New York

We need to understand what the other parts of the society need from us.

— Francesco Starace, former ENEL Group CEO

COVID-19 has also deepened the erosion of trust in traditional institutions … but businesses have an opportunity to lead. Employees are increasingly looking to their employer as the most trusted competent, and ethical source of information … Putting your company's purpose at the foundation of your relationships with your stakeholders is critical to long-term success.

— Larry Fink, Chairman & CEO BlackRock

Introduction

The world today is characterized by an imbalance among four key democratic constituencies: governments, corporations, the media, and non-governmental organizations (NGOs). Among these four pillars, the public impression of competence and influence, and the respect it engenders, has tilted in favor of corporations, according to recent surveys such as the 2023 Edelman Trust Barometer.[1]

Governments are struggling to respond to new crises and people's needs, while the media are mostly polarized and have lost the traditional equidistance that once made them reliable and trustworthy. NGOs have a more limited purpose, fulfilling specific roles and providing services.

The inability of governments to intermediate effectively between diverse and often conflicting interests has turned up the pressure on corporations to engage proactively for the common good and to fill some of the voids left by an ill attended policymaking.

Corporations need a new operating model to adapt to a societal context in which policymakers need to be continuously and deeply informed about increasingly complex, technologically intensive, and ethically charged issues. At the same time, corporations need a more educated general public to set the expectations for how a business can operate in today's world.

The Influence, Relevance & Growth (IRG) system offers insight and a methodology for companies to manage this new complex environment. By virtue of the trust enjoyed today by corporations, IRG helps them

---

[1] 2023 Edelman Trust Barometer.

understand if they are fit and aligned to respond to this heightened level of expectations.

The IRG methodology was developed by Newest in collaboration with Kearney, a top management consulting firm, and Symanto, an Artificial Intelligence company specialized in insights generation.

Based on 10 quantitative parameters, it assigns a score from 1 to 30 (perfect score), allowing an organization to identify where it needs to improve in order to reach a score of 20. In fact above this threshold (according to the IRG metrics) the company can be considered able to express its influence and play a relevant role, ultimately contributing to overall economic growth.

This approach allows a corporation to adapt and transfer knowledge to both policymakers and the community at large to help address the most pressing societal issues and those related to its core business.

Far from suggesting that corporations get involved in politics, the IRG's goal is to help companies adapt to this new, out-of-sync environment and help them to inform policy. In particular, organizations will be able to better define the boundaries of possible actions and to avoid being drawn into politics, which remains the core business of elected officials.

This book analyzes what has driven the rise of business and proposes a pragmatic and measurable set of actions to help companies adapt to societal changes, support policymakers, manage new stakeholder expectations, and continue to generate economic growth while protecting shareholder value.

The Russian Federation's invasion of Ukraine and military maneuvers around Taiwan, have added an unanticipated layer of complexity for policymakers and a business world already grappling with the Covid-19 pandemic and climate change, among other issues. Combined with other fundamental transformations in international and national society, a new vision of the Western world will be critical. Value chains will have to be redesigned and new legislation conceived. How the business world interacts with policymakers in these unprecedented times will be critical to the continued success of Western society, and to those elsewhere who aspire to its benefits.

The book is divided into six chapters: Chapter I provides two brief overviews: of the IRG and of the current state of Western society; Chapters II and III explain the background and need for this approach; Chapter IV illustrates the early Stages of Corporate Social Responsibility (CSR); Chapter V analyzes the evolution – and the limits – of the overstretched adoption of ESG (Environmental, Social, and Governance criteria) for corporate decision makers, while Chapter VI expands on the methodology of shaping the influence, relevance & growth of corporations in a rapidly changing world.

From the end of World War II to the present day, the book examines critical moments marked by the rise and fall of the primacy of politics, leading to the high level of trust that corporations enjoy today. The history presented here is neither mechanistic nor deterministic, and a full accounting of past events helps to identify measurable solutions while acquainting us with the admirable strengths and the perils of our own culture.

1 Business as Usual: The Twentieth Century

1.1 The Influence, Relevance & Growth of Corporations in a Changing World

In the West, we are out of sync with our four key democratic constituents: governments, corporations, NGOs, and the media.

These play a critical role in democracies, where there is a system of separation of powers and of checks and balances.

In a democracy, the people express their sovereignty through a process of free elections. The winners, in turn, are legitimized to form a government that will implement the platform or set of policies on which they were elected. The government represents the executive power and acts in the name and on behalf of all citizens. From this legitimacy comes the primacy of politics, the duty to make proposals to Parliament, the legislative power, and to provide a vision and to implement policies that effectively mediate between divergent or conflicting interests in a synthesis that promotes social cohesion and the economic development of a country. Competence and in-depth understanding of the issues at hand that need to be regulated are, among other things, necessary traits of the primacy of politics. Furthermore, being democracy a delicate construct, it requires informed citizens, and "it asks" from its political leaders "for good faith and restraints, and a willingness to put the collective interest before politics, party, or personal gain."[1]

---

[1] Richard Haass, *The Bill of Obligations. The Ten Habits of Good Citizens*, Penguin Press, 2023.

Corporations are large companies or a group of companies authorized to act as a single entity and recognized as such by law. A company can be publicly listed, state- owned or held privately by its shareholders. Companies are essential to the creation of wealth, jobs, and to the well-being of all stakeholders, not just shareholders. To compete and excel companies hire the best and the brightest. As we will see, over the past 30 years, corporations have grown in size, competence, and financial strength, largely monopolizing the pool of available talent at the expense of the public sector and governments in democracies. To fulfill their mission, companies need a stable and predictable environment, as well as traits of openness and alignment with the structural changes that have occurred in society to play a leading and informing role.

NGOs[2] are non-profit organizations that operate independently of any government, usually to address a social, political, or humanitarian issue. Universities and trade unions can also be considered NGOs. They are funded through extensive and ongoing fundraising campaigns. Often formed to fulfill purposes based on individual life experiences, NGOs represent a vast and atomized archipelago of entities that rarely merge. They proliferate in democracies and, depending on their scope, even operate in non-democratic regimes as agents of positive change. To fulfill their mission, NGOs must maintain traits of independence and selflessness and strive for the common good.

The fourth key component of democracy is the media, the main means of mass communication (broadcasting, publishing, Internet). The media are essential democratic assets that provide access to information. This is critical to the health and resilience of democracy for two main reasons, in the words of the U.S. Agency for International Development: *"First, it ensures that citizens make responsible, informed choices rather than acting out of ignorance or misinformation. Second, information serves a 'checking function' by ensuring that elected representatives uphold their oaths of office and carry out the wishes of those who elected them. In some societies, an antagonistic relationship between media and government represents a vital and healthy element of fully functioning de-*

---

[2] Many NGOs are active in humanitarianism or the social sciences; they may also include clubs and associations that provide services to their members and others. NGOs can also be corporate lobbying groups, such as the World Economic Forum.

mocracies."[3] Independence, objectivity, factuality, fairness and balance, among others, are necessary traits for the reliability, trust, and reputation of the media.

While these four constituencies are vital to any democracy, they require that the traits outlined above be present and recognized by all.

Democracies are fragile constructs. The Democracy Index provides an interesting snapshot of how democracies can slide into a more flawed system. The four constituencies illustrated earlier are critical to the performance of five activities essential to democracy: the electoral process and pluralism, the functioning of government, political participation, political culture, and civil liberties. Close to half of the world's population (Fig. 1.1) lives in some form of democracy, nearly half of the world's population (45.3%). However, only 8% live in a "best performing democracy," compared to 8.9% in 2015, before the U.S. was downgraded to a "democracy with some downsides" in 2016 (Fig. 1.2).[4]

Figure 1.1 Types Regimes classification in 2022

Cluster	Number of Countries	% of Countries	% of World Population
1. Democracies (best performers)	24	14.4	8.0
2. Democracies (with some downsides)	48	28.7	37.3
3. Regimes (in between in clusters 2 and 4)	36	21.6	17.9
4. Autocracy, despotism, dictatorship, totalitarianism, and monocracy	59	35.3	36.9

Note: "World" population refers to the total population of the 167 countries and territories covered by the Index. Since this excludes only microstates, it is close to the total estimated world population.

Source: Adapted by the author from Economist Intelligence Unit, *Democracy Index 2022*

---

[3] Center for Democracy and Governance Bureau for Global Programs, Field Support, and Research U.S. Agency for International Development, *The Role of Media in Democracy: A Strategic Approach*, June 1999.

[4] Source: EIU, Democracy Index 2022.

In this regard, it is interesting to compare the world's best-performing democracy, Norway, with the United States and to appreciate its democratic shortcomings, particularly in the functioning of government.

Figure 1.2 Comparing Best performing World's Democracy vs USA

	Overall Score	Rank	Electoral Process & Pluralism	Functioning of Government	Political Participation	Political Culture	Civil Liberties
Norway*	9.81	1	10	9.64	10	10	9.41
USA**	7.85	0	9.17	6.43	8.89	6.25	8.53

Notes: * population 5.5 million, 2023 yearly growth 0.74%; ** population 340 million, 2023 yearly growth 0.5%

Source: Adapted by the author from Worldmeter and Economist Intelligence Unit, *Democracy Index 2022*

These data help introduce one of the essential elements that has driven the thinking behind IRG: trust. In this regard, Edelman, a privately held global communications firm, launched the "Edelman Trust Barometer"[5] in 2001. By surveying people in 28 countries, this tool annually assesses the level of trust in four key institutions: Business, NGOs, Government, and Media (survey results are listed below). The 2023 Trust Barometer shows that trust in government is low and, together with the media, it is the least trusted institution.[6]

Figure 1.3 Overall Trust in the 4 Institutions (Global 27) 2023

	Business	NGOs	Government	Media
Trust	62	59	50	50
Change 2022 to 2023	-1	**-1**	-1	**-2**

Legend: 60-100 Trust; 50-59 Neutral; 1-49 Distrust; Bold: significant change

Source: Adapted by the author from 2023 Edelman Trust Barometer

---

 [5] The 2023 Edelman Trust Barometer is based on 28 countries surveyed, 32.000+ interviews, 1.1150+ respondents per country.
 [6] 2023 Edelman Trust Barometer.

Figure 1.4 Trust in Government in 28 Countries, 2023

Country	Trust in Governments	Change 2022 to 2023
China	89	-2
UAE	86	-1
Saudi Arabia	83	+1
India	76	+2
Indonesia	76	0
Singapore	76	+2
Sweden	57	NA
France	56	+3
Thailand	56	-4
Malaysia	54	-8
Canada	51	-2
The Netherlands	51	-7
Germany	47	0
Ireland	47	-2
Mexico	47	+4
Italy	46	-3
Australia	45	-7
Kenya	43	+4
USA	42	+3
Brazil	40	**+6**
Colombia	40	**+8**
UK	37	-5
Spain	36	+2
Nigeria	35	+1
South Korea	34	**-8**
Japan	33	-3
South Africa	22	-4
Argentina	20	-2

Legend: 60-100 Trust; 50-59 Neutral; 1-49 Distrust; Bold: significant change

Source: Adapted by the author from 2023 Edelman Trust Barometer

The Edelman Trust Barometer supports the notion that the four institutions are out of balance and, most importantly, that democratic governments have lost their essential traits by failing to exercise the primacy of politics. In other words, "elected officials" do not enjoy the trust or the confidence of the electorate.

In a balanced society, governments are trusted because they effectively mediate between conflicting interests and contribute to the stability and predictability of a given socio-economic environment.

Public perceptions of competence and ethics, and the respect they engender, have shifted significantly in favor of corporations.[7] Business must now step forward and fill the void, even though they were not designed to do so.

In fact, respondents to the 2023 Edelman Trust Barometer expect CEOs to take a public stand on the issues listed in Figure 1.5.

Figure 1.5   CEOs Expected to Act (Global 27)

Issues	Percentage Who Say
Treatment of Employees	89%
Climate Change	82%
Discrimination	80%
Wealth Gap	77%
Immigration	72%

Source: Adapted by the author from 2023 Edelman Trust Barometer

Business is best at creating value for shareholders, as an engine of innovation, and as a driver of economic prosperity. But in today's rapidly changing social context and heightened expectations, a company's expanded mission should include creating value and sharing knowledge with the full range of stakeholders – owners, employees, consumers, policymakers, and society at large. Moreover, anticipating, managing, and delivering on such expectations will ensure and solidify continued value

---

[7] Source: 2023 Edelman Trust Barometer.

creation for shareholders while clarifying to stakeholders that there are limits to what companies can do.

According to respondents to the 2023 Edelman Trust Barometer,[8] CEOs have an obligation to:

Figure 1.6 CEOs Obligations

Topic	Percentage Who Say
Defend facts and expose questionable science used to justify bad social policy	72%
Pull advertising money from platforms that spread misinformation	71%
Companies could strengthen the social fabric if they Support politicians and media that build consensus and cooperation (avg)	64%

Note: Global 25 excluding China and Thailand
Source: 2023 Edelman Trust Barometer

This requires skills and processes that go beyond traditional communications or lobbying to ensure a receptive understanding of corporate plans as they become more complex and technologically intensive. If a company's positioning is misunderstood, its actions can become controversial.

The goal of the Influence, Relevance & Growth approach and methodology is to help companies that operate in democracies – full or flawed – to recognize this imbalance and to engineer ways to compensate for policy shortcomings by proactively sharing and transferring know-how to policymakers and the public at large.

According to the IRG, business must inform politics, not enter it.

In fact, Edelman Trust Barometer respondents affirm that the best societal outcomes on the most pressing societal issues (averaged across climate change, discrimination, immigration, treatment of workers, and income inequality) are achieved when government and business work together.

---

[8] 2023 Edelman Trust Barometer.

Figure 1.7   Government and Business Modus Operandi

Modus Operandi	Percentage Who Say
Government & Business working in partnership	41% (4X more likely to yield optimal results from partnership than business alone)
Both working independently	21%
Government only working alone	16%
Business only working alone	10%

Note: Global 25 excluding China and Thailand

Source: 2023 Edelman Trust Barometer

The IRG recognizes and manages the structural changes taking place in society. It provides companies with the tools they need, including:

- Measuring broader influence. Building the company's gravitas and positional strength through its status and competencies to support and help shape policy.
- Strengthen capability. Ensuring that the company can openly and transparently build consensus and support for strategic issues, whether core or tangential, that require deeper understanding and appreciation.
- Increasing relevance. Becoming a valued and sought-after intermediary for policymakers, and socially valued by consumers and employees.
- Leadership and governance. Improving management capabilities to avoid being overwhelmed by increasing stakeholder expectations on new issues not related to the core business or tangential to it.
- Risk control. Reducing the risks associated with implementing strategic plans.
- Growth. Creating robust long-term value for sharefolders.

The IRG system, and this book, is aimed at two main groups:

The first group are CEOs and top management – and those who aspire to these positions – who are struggling today to align their companies with the changing social structure in response to the high level of trust. With leadership comes responsibility. A new culture, DNA, and skillset are needed to become partners with policymakers in addressing the most pressing societal and industry issues. As we will see later in this book, the technological complexity and, at times, the ethical challenges posed by the conquest of new frontiers – such as artificial intelligence (AI), biogenetics, regenerative medicine, etc. – require policymakers to have the competence and understanding of these issues if companies are to operate in stable and predictable markets.

The second group are business students. The changes and shifts in spheres of influence and competence among the four constituencies appear to be structural, at least for the foreseeable future. Students will benefit from a reading of society that offers a more realistic perspective, one that clearly shows how an overshadowed primacy of politics can be compensated by the corporate world. In addition, as the title of this book suggests, students need to be prepared for a world that goes beyond the ESG and learn how a company can adapt to this new environment while setting expectations to avoid being drawn into politics.

Where the IRG has been applied in practice – for example, in the energy, pharmaceutical, and transportation sectors – top management has found its methodology and metrics to be instrumental in gaining insight and an orderly assessment of a company's impact, relevance, and potential. Executives have learned how to increase these metrics through a selection of programs that enhance their company's gravitas and prestige.

One top executive from the energy industry commented:

"At the beginning I thought this was the nth consulting intellectual extravaganza. On the contrary the IRG provided order, crystallized an enhanced understanding of our purpose and how to lead the external expectations. The action plan coherently and pragmatically drove us in reaching this goal."[9]

This approach is particularly timely as governments around the world are called upon to reshape a world disrupted by the intersection of war, pandemics, global warming, inequality, inflation, and other hurdles. The International Monetary Fund (IMF) recently described the current global situation as a "confluence of calamities." The invasion of Ukraine unexpectedly united liberal democratic governments in their response, and many companies withdrew from Russia in anticipation of, or in response

---

[9] Name and organization withheld for reasons of confidentiality.

to their customers' expectations. The war thus brought an added sense of urgency to finding a new operating model to resolve the confluence of so many overlapping and inescapable problems. Many governments are realizing that this gathering storm of global crises cannot be solved in isolation. Expectations for institutions to join forces to provide compelling and sustainable answers have never been higher.

Increasingly, the long-term prospects of companies are only as healthy as the societies and environments in which they operate. By applying the proposed IRG metrics, companies can not only reduce the risk to their operations, but also benefit in terms of corporate reputation and the bottom line.

1.2   The Past and the Primacy of Politics

In the years following World War II, the political leaders of the victorious nations decided to organize the world to ensure reconstruction, peace, and inclusive economic growth. In the later years of the Cold War, Western leaders reinforced this governance to ensure the resilience of capitalism and, ultimately, its victory over Soviet communism.

Up to a point in history, and partly in the service of that victory, Western political systems effectively and equitably mediated between the interests of capital and the general welfare of the population. In this balance, corporations stood behind elected officials who met the challenges of the time with competence and foresight. NGOs were in their infancy. The political system was, for the most part, effective in responding to the needs of society. The Internet did not exist, and the media – consisting mainly of television, radio, and newspapers – were not atomized: the largely neutral, responsible, and trustworthy Fourth Estate.

1.2.1   *Corporate Leadership and the Present*

Today, thirty years after the fall of the Berlin Wall and in the midst of an unexpected war on European soil, we live in an era of multiple threats to the democratic system.

In 1992 Francis Fukuyama published his book *The End of History and the Last Man*. He argued that the end of the Cold War meant that liberalism would triumph across the planet. In 1996 Samuel Huntington published a response, *The Clash of Civilizations*, in which he stated that liberalism would not triumph by stopping history, but that in the future, blocs of spiritual and religious civilizations would become the engines of the continuation of history. A number of subsequent events, such as the terrorist attacks of September 11, 2001, have shown Huntington to be more in tune with the times than Fukuyama.

It is easy to understand Fukuyama's optimistic perspective, for the 1990s was a period of extreme euphoria. Partly in the wake of break-through technologies, liberal democracies privatized formerly state-owned enterprises and liberalized most industries. Politics began to lose ground, and many questioned whether the "costs" of politics were even necessary; the projected scenario of a global, self-regulated, seamless marketplace served by the Internet raised questions about the possibility of rationalizing the costs associated with regulators and politicians. The eminent US political commentator Thomas L. Friedman wrote a best-selling book, *The World Is Flat*, an analysis of globalization at the turn of the century, a metaphor for seeing the world as a level playing field for commerce: all competitors, except for labor, had equal opportunities.

In this context, the business world has undergone a profound transformation over the same period. Companies have achieved unprecedented wealth, scale, and geopolitical influence. They have acquired cutting-edge skills and sophisticated management systems. In the process, corporations have largely, if not exclusively, monopolized the pool of available talent. By contrast, the public sector remains on the margins of globalization. It has lost three decades of basic know-how that is essential for effective mediation between the interests of capital and the well-being of the population.

Populism is to a large extent the offspring of this lack of mediation. It combines with other troublesome aspects of a weakened democratic world at a moment when history, which we were told had ended, is re-surfacing.

1.2.2 *From the Past to the Future, from CSR to ESG and then IRG*

In the 1970s the idea of Corporate Social Responsibility (CSR) was an early attempt to help U.S. corporations become more responsible members of the communities in which they operated. CSR soon became a standard practice around the world, and companies welcomed the CSR imprimatur as a means of changing negative perceptions of a their activities. The stakeholder concept was born: anyone directly or indirectly affected by the company's activities should be considered. Noble in spirit, in practice CSR operated from two basic defensive perspectives. It developed public relations strategies to engage with these new stakeholder constituencies and to advise on potential risks in the implementation of corporate actions. At the same time, it sought to identify potentially hostile elements within these new constituencies and to identify potential disruptive issues that might affect the core business.

In recent years, CSR has evolved to include sustainability, or ESG (Environmental, Social, and Governance) criteria. ESG provides a set of standards by which investors concerned about environmental issues and other concerns can screen potential investments. It is also increasingly seen as a public metric. ESG is the latest iteration of what was once called "stakeholder capitalism," a management system that directs corporations to serve the interests not only of shareholders – who seek for a financial return on their investment in the firm – but also of customers, suppliers, employees, local communities, and society at large.[10]

This new wave of ESG-driven stakeholder capitalism has been endorsed by both the World Economic Forum and the Business Roundtable.[11] Tackling the challenge of global warming has become paramount, steering the world toward new energy horizons that favor renewables. ESG practices now span the entire business world. By the end of 2021, 13% ($8.4 trillion) of the $66 trillion in professionally managed assets in the United States will be invested in sustainable assets.[12] The significance of this amount can be measured against the 2022 U.S. GDP of $25.4 trillion.

These practices are commendable and have raised the visibility of companies and corporate leaders on pressing issues that have languished due to a lack of system and interface. Business leaders have realized that addressing and working on such issues makes a difference. These same

----

[10] ESG Enterprise.

[11] Business Roundtable is an association of America's CEOs working to promote a thriving U.S. economy and expanded opportunity for all Americans through sound public policy.

[12] US SIF Foundation, 2022 Trends Reports.

practices, however, have inspired ideological positions by politicians and commentators, and have sometimes been misused as "greenwashing," a practice whereby business operations continue as usual but are given an undeserved or unearned environmental spin, as many studies show.

In terms of culture and process, ESG can be said to have laid a solid foundation within the organizations that have adopted it. However, ESG functions as an audit, an internal system of corporate controls. It has not been built as a response to the fundamental changes that are rapidly occurring in a societal context: the immense structural disruptions that are underway and inevitable in the near future. We are witnessing, among other things, the decline of the state as an actor that has lost the primacy of politics legitimized by democratic elections, the media crisis of polarization and fake news, and the increasingly insistent demands of stakeholders for greater social engagement by CEOs.

While ESG has been a welcome improvement over unfettered capitalism in its own arena, it has not contributed to rebalancing the four pillars discussed above. Nor, crucially, has it identified a new system through which to cooperate proactively with policymakers and other constituencies. This is a fundamental necessity given the structural shift in the population with respect to the key aspect of trust. ESG is praised, but it is also becoming a source of political polarization. In the United States, for example, Republican attorneys general in 19 states have accused Black-Rock, an asset management company, of abusing its influence and power by boycotting fossil fuel companies. Blackrock disagrees and denies the allegations. At the same time, watchdogs in New York, a Democratic state, complain that the same asset manager is not green enough. What's more, Texas is rumored to be considering banning its pension funds from doing business with BlackRock. The bottom line is that ESG does not proactively address broader imbalances.

In the case of large corporations, the concerns of the general public are no longer necessarily expressed exclusively through the ballot box. These calls to action are landing on CEO's desks with increasing insistence through activism, boycotts, and the disruption of normal business operations due to global social and environmental crises. What is needed is a more proactive corporate strategy, capable of building solid, dynamic, and effective bridges with other constituencies, while also limiting the scope of expectations that sometimes transcend the business world and are in fact political demands.

While no methodology can anticipate a "black swan" event such as the invasion of Ukraine, this conflict makes a post-war economic, social, and geopolitical soft landing all the more urgent. One of the ways in which the IRG supports the orderly realization of this future is by promoting the exchange of knowledge and skills between companies and policymakers.

A brief look at cloning, one aspect of a rapidly accelerating new future, serves to illustrate how a complicated and ethically charged intersection between business and society will need to be mediated. It was headline news in 1996 when a sheep named Dolly became the first mammal to be cloned from an adult somatic cell. Today, the average price of cloning a pet in the United States is $35,000, down more than 60% from 2010 and a fraction Dolly's cost. While the wealthy once sought immortality through art, today these resources are being invested in the field of regenerative medicine. Cloning, hibernation, bioengineering and neural chips are just some of the new technologies aimed at extending life expectancy and preserving and even regenerating youth.

Science fiction is becoming science fact at an extraordinary rate, with potentially profound social, cultural, and anthropological implications. Yuval Noah Harari, author of the best-selling book *Sapiens*, speculates in his follow-up, *Homo Deus: A Brief History of Tomorrow*, that such advances mean that the human species could become two separate species within a short time, as those who can afford to be enhanced begin to breed a new type of human being.

Cloning, if properly managed, can be a benign science, as can the potentially more consequential fields of robotics and artificial intelligence. But at the same time, we can look to the factionalizing effects of unmanaged social media, with its relatively primitive AI, for a glimpse of what an unmanaged future would look like. Policymakers will be called upon to regulate these extraordinarily complex arenas of both opportunity and threat. This dialogue should be intensified now so that these policymakers can make informed decisions. What applies to these new medical advances also applies to a range of other industries, so it is essential that companies share their expertise to help policymakers shape and manage this new future as the public becomes more informed.

On the culturally evolving human, the UN reports that nearly half of the world's population is under the age of thirty, and that "the private sector is the main driver in the fight against poverty, providing 9 out of 10 jobs." Generation Z, those born since 1997[13], make up 30% of the world's population and, along with the Millennials who preceded them, will soon make up the majority of the workforce and the consumer ecosystem. Gen Z represents an evolution of Millennials' "conscious consumption" – the tech-savvy, socially conscious mind. It is a transnational, global sensibility, inclusive, tolerant, and responsible; Gen Z's guiding metrics are ethics, social responsibility and brand diversity. Wherever located, they are individualistic and capitalistic, but this is now a constant two-way conversation. They have a communal sensibility, "influencing" is central to their information ecosystem, and they are globally instant in their communications.

So, the previously unspoken need that has been brewing in societies is now becoming loud and insistent. Key questions arise: are CEOs aware of these tectonic shifts in society? Are they ready for the new role the public is demanding of them? Social market research shows that employees and stakeholders have this expectation, and 74% of respondents in the Edelman Trust Barometer say that CEOs should lead change and not wait for government to impose it. Furthermore, in 2021, 86% of respondents say that CEOs should publicly speak on pandemic impact, job automation, societal issues and local community issues.[14] It is an expectation that demands a response for the good of all. For the good of the CEO and the company, it requires intelligent management.

1.2.3 *Influence, Relevance and Growth*

In 2003, I teamed up with three of my former partners at the management consulting firm Booz Allen Hamilton to ask how to manage a post-globalized world – by and large characterized by inequalities due to offshoring, smart sourcing practices, and the rise of China. Our book *Megacommunities*, published in 2008, was the result.[15] We conducted a global consultation, interviewing one hundred leaders from government, business, and NGOs, to create an early organizational framework for an

---

[13] *"Some sources give the specific year range of 1997–2012, although the years spanned are sometimes contested or debated because generations and their zeitgeists are difficult to delineate"* Source: britannica.com

[14] Data are from 2021 Edelman Trust Barometer, p. 35.

[15] Gerencser M., Van Lee R., Napolitano F., Kelly C., *Megacommunities: How Leaders of Government, Business and Non-Profits Can Tackle Today's Global Challenges Together*, St. Martin's Publishing Group, 2008.

increasingly globalized and interconnected world. We called for a new kind of tri-sector leadership, one in which business, government, and nonprofits work together, through continuous negotiation and collaboration on shared prosperity goals.

One of the key lessons that my colleagues and I have learned from this approach is that such systems need to be proactive in order to be truly effective. So in developing the IRG, the goal was to create an actionable system that takes into account the shift in competencies that now favors corporations. The problems of society are no longer separate from the problems of business. All employees need to understand and support the strategic charters of the companies they work for and their impact on the broader social context. Customers also want to understand what a company stands for and whether those positions align with their values. Suppliers look to the companies they work with as role models to learn from and emulate. Shareholders, while awaiting their returns, are increasingly attentive to the company's place and vision in society. Policymakers need to be competent and informed about the world's evolutions and complexities.

The IRG considers ten pragmatic, measurable parameters and, as noted earlier, incorporates ESG. It adds consideration of the intersection between the company and policymakers, assessing areas where closer collaboration could help policymakers and also benefit the company. In this way, it measures how a company can, and should, become influential and relevant outside of traditional industry parameters.

It is important to emphasize that the IRG does not advocate that companies get involved in politics. Rather, the role is to assist, transfer knowledge and help policymakers ensure the social and environmental stability in which business can continue to thrive.

To do this, companies need processes of cognition and depth that allow them to implement strategic plans with the necessary thoroughness of knowledge about these sensitive issues. The company should be confident in its evolving understanding; it should be able to explain it effectively to the public; and it should be able to work with policymakers to help them anticipate, understand, and address complicated factors before they escalate.

1.2.4 *A Fundamental Change*

The Russian invasion of Ukraine has endangered the system of international rules and laws – globalization – which until February 2022 was respected by political and economic actors alike, regardless of whether they were democracies or totalitarian regimes. Russia and Ukraine, with their economic and financial assets, are now outside this system. Other totalitarian regimes, such as China or Turkey, were lukewarm in their condemnation of the Russians' violation of international law, if not silent. This episode endangered the reliability and security of production, raw material procurement and transportation. "Friend-shoring," "near-shoring," "reshoring" and "onshoring" are new terms describing a world disrupted by the war on European soil. The U.S. government intends to source components and raw materials from "friendly" countries with shared value to boost the security of domestic production.

The ability to organize global supply chains based solely on cost-benefit parameters is less certain today, and all commercial relationships are under scrutiny. These structural changes call for the private sector to adapt by broadening its positioning, perspective, language and actions, and acquiring the skills that this new business ecosystem requires. In the United States, the CEO of JP Morgan Chase was already advocating and pursuing the same path, and made this explicit in his letter to shareholders in March 2019:

1. *The third section is about American public policy ... I try to give a comprehensive, multi-year overview of what I see as some of our problems and suggest a few ways they can be addressed ... American public policy ... is a major concern: businesses, governments, and communities need to work as partners, collaboratively and constructively, to analyze and solve problems and help strengthen the economy for everyone's benefit. The American Dream is alive — but fraying for many.*

2. *We must have a proper diagnosis of our problems — the issues are real and serious — if we want to have the proper prescription that leads to workable solutions.*

3. *All these issues are fixable, but that will happen only if we set aside partisan politics and narrow self-interest — our country must come first.*

4. *Governments must be better and more effective — we cannot succeed without their help. The rest of us could do a better job, too.*

5. *CEOs: Your country needs you!*

6. *America's global role and engagement are indispensable.*

On August 19, 2019, the Business Roundtable, a coalition of 181 CEOs of American companies, signed the "Statement on the Purpose of a Corporation" which follows this line and philosophy.[16] Finally, the Edelman Trust Barometer advises that "business must embrace its expanded mandate and expectations, with CEOs leading on a range of familiar and unfamiliar issues. It's important to take meaningful action first and then communicate about it."

---

[16] https://www.businessroundtable.org/business-roundtable-redefines-the-purpose-of-a-corporation-to-promote-an-economy-that-serves-all-americans

2   The Past and the Primacy of Politics

Many, including young business students, have not lived in a balanced society where governments are competent and respected. To this end, it is appropriate to take a brief look at the recent past to highlight the intense changes that have already happened, the speed with which they have occurred, and the profound transformations in society that have resulted.

The 1990s were an extraordinary period of economic growth, euphoria, and a deeply shared belief that the future would be better, more interesting, and more generous. At the turn of the millennium, however, protest movements grew as people around the world began to question globalization. On November 30, 1999, members of the World Trade Organization (WTO) convened in Seattle to launch a new round of trade negotiations. A major protest coincided with this meeting, the size of which, estimated at 40,000 demonstrators, dwarfed any such previous demonstration in the United States against a world meeting of any of the organizations generally associated with economic globalization.[1] The massive and violent street protests – dubbed the "Battle of Seattle" – dominated the mainstream media headlines rather than the negotiations, and the message was clear.[2]

Opponents of globalization argued that it only served the interests of U.S. multinationals and corporations at the expense of the domestic population and the Third World. They argued that it increased poverty and

---

[1] The Seattle Police Department After Action Report: November 29 – December 3, 1999. p. 41. "Police estimated the size of this march [the labor march] in excess of 40,000."

[2] britannica.com/event/Seattle-WTO-protests-of-1999

worsened income inequality. In essence, Western political systems began – at different paces – to abdicate their roles as intermediaries between the interests of capital and the well-being of the population at large, both at home and abroad. Their influence and relevance began to wane.

On the other hand, globalization had in fact leveraged the practices and ethos of a political system that in previous decades had wisely and competently designed and created the institutions that ensured peace, stability, and predictability. These are critical components of the environment that businesses need to invest and prosper.

While the world is not new to globalization, the pace of the current round, which began in the early 1990s after the fall of the Berlin Wall, has been particularly rapid and disruptive.[3] This acceleration has taken political and other systems by surprise and disrupted the balance between the four components of the Western social context: governments, corporations, media, and NGOs.

One statistic illustrates the pace and consequences. In 2003, 29 of the 100 largest economies in the world were corporations, not countries (based on GDP). By 2020, companies will account for 40 of the top 100 economies, with total revenues of $ 8 trillion. The IMF estimated global GDP in 2020 at $83 trillion, meaning that forty companies accounted for 10% of the global economy. In 2003, the largest company was oil producer Exxon, with revenues of $178.9 billion, ranking it 45th in the world, roughly the size of Pakistan's economy. In 2020, Walmart was the largest company in the world in terms of revenue, with sales of $549 billion. This placed Walmart 24th in the world, larger than Sweden, whose GDP is $529 billion. From a capitalization perspective, FAANG (Facebook, Apple, Amazon, Netflix, Google) boast $9 trillion, which, due to the nature of their respective businesses, gives this cluster a significant level of influence and power over world affairs.

Several factors, including the end of the Cold War, the expansion of capital markets, and liberalization and privatization, have helped globalization thrive and endure. A critical element of the difference from previous eras of globalization is that this one was governed by the rule of law; no war was waged to set it in motion. Beginning in 1945, political leaders

---

[3] The first period of globalization was the Late Bronze Age, a thriving inter-kingdom system of trade in the Mediterranean which suffered a catastrophic collapse circa 1,200 BCE into a subsequent 'dark age'.

in Brussels, Geneva, New York, and Washington created enduring global institutions that fostered dialogue, established common military defense systems, and created mechanisms for resolving disputes. As a result, a stable, negotiated environment was created in which economic growth could be financed across borders.

Again, history matters, and what follows is a bird's-eye view of the legitimacy and competence that are required to lead public opinion and to establish transnational institutions critical to the maintenance of global order, peace, and respect for international law.

The United Nations is a model of such principles. Founded in 1945, it was built on the lessons learned from the failures of its predecessor, the League of Nations, which had failed to prevent Axis aggression in the 1930s, culminating in World War II. The League's credibility was weak because the United States never became a member, and the Soviet Union joined late, soon to be expelled after invading Finland. Germany, Japan, Italy, Spain, and others also withdrew from the League. The UN, by contrast, set a standard of commitment by the victorious powers of World War II that would prove indispensable during the Cold War. Liberal democracies could be in a constant state of negotiation with totalitarian regimes.

In his 2017 book *A World in Disarray*, Richard Haass notes, "One of the many ironies of history [is that] much of what constituted international order in the second half of the twentieth century was forged with a non-democratic, non-market society that was an adversary of the United States."[4] Through such postwar institutions and principles, dialogue was maintained and the possibility of a devastating nuclear confrontation between the United States and the Soviet Union became remote, notwithstanding the Cuban Missile Crisis of 1962.[5]

Learning from the harsh terms of settlement of World War I, which devastated and humiliated Germany and set it on the path to Nazism, U.S. foreign aid to Western Europe in 1947 took the form of the Mar-

---

[4] Richard Haass, *A World in Disarray*, Penguin Books, 2017, p.37.
[5] The Cuban Missile Crisis of 1962 was a confrontation lasting one month and four days (16 October – 20 November 1962) between the US and the Soviet Union which escalated into an international crisis when American deployments of missiles in Italy and Turkey were matched by Soviet deployments of similar ballistic missiles in Cuba.

shall Plan, officially the European Recovery Program. Between April 1948 and June 1951, the United States transferred $13.2 billion, the equivalent of $160 billion in today's dollars, to help sixteen countries get back on their feet. The Marshall Plan is deservedly legendary for its vision and accomplishments.[6] It made Europe a solid economic player and helped create and nurture liberal democracies – including in Germany and Italy – setting the stage for the economic boom of the 1960s.

Other international organizations and agreements are also noteworthy. In 1944, the International Monetary Fund was created to promote international monetary cooperation, exchange rate stability and orderly exchange arrangements, while fostering economic growth to generate high levels of employment. Meanwhile, the World Bank focused on fighting poverty and improving the living standards of people in the developing countries. In addition, the General Agreement on Tariffs and Trade (GATT) was signed by twenty-three nations in Geneva on October 30, 1947. Its purpose was to promote international trade by reducing or eliminating trade barriers such as tariffs and quotas. Finally, the World Trade Organization (WTO) was established as permanent body in Geneva in 1995.

In the area of common defense, the North Atlantic Treaty Organization (NATO) was established in 1949 as a military alliance against a possible Soviet invasion of Western Europe. It now consists of thirty European and North American countries. NATO is a system of collective defense in which independent member states agree to mutual defense if attacked by an outside party. Soon after the Russian invasion of Ukraine, Sweden and Finland joined NATO as well.

In 1975, the Group of 7 (G7) was formed under the leadership of French President Valéry Giscard d'Estaing. Representing their respective nations, the elected officials led while the other constituencies stayed on their own course. The G7 is an intergovernmental political forum consisting of Canada, France, Germany, Italy, Japan, the United Kingdom, and the United States. Its members are the world's largest advanced economies and wealthiest liberal democracies. The group is formally organized around shared values such as pluralism and representative gov-

---

[6] Council on Foreign Relations, «It Takes More Than Money to Make a Marshall Plan», Blog Post by Benn Steil and Benjamin Della Rocca, April 9, 2018 10:00 pm (EST).

ernment. As of 2018, the G7 nations accounted for nearly 60 percent of global net wealth, or $317 trillion.[7]

Today, G7 leadership is no longer able to shape the global economy as it once could. The days when finance ministers and central bankers could design and lead bold, far-reaching global policy changes are long gone. For example, on September 22, 1985, faced with an overvalued U.S. dollar, the finance ministers of the world's five largest economies announced the "Plaza Accords" to devalue the dollar against the French franc, the German deutsche mark, the Japanese yen, and the British pound by intervening in currency markets to correct the imbalance. By the end of 1987, the dollar had fallen 54% from its peak. This is an example of cooperative concerted action on a global scale that produced successful results with negligible instability.

This is not to be nostalgic. There is no question that these international institutions have become increasingly ineffective. They reflect their formative period, when they were designed to prevent and suppress future disruption and aggression by hostile leaders or countries. Precisely because of this grand geopolitical vision, they have become resistant to change and difficult to reform. Moreover, they have come to be seen as remote and irrelevant to the immediate concerns of the public. The United Nations Security Council is an example of this stasis. Its permanent membership was created after the Second World War: China, France, Russia, the United Kingdom, and the United States. The fact that leading economic players such as Germany, Japan or India are not permanent members makes the institution seem archaic.

The United Nations Climate Change Conference in Glasgow in 2021, also known as COP26, sought to commit participants to higher ambitions to mitigate climate change. While, as usual in these cases, there are supporters and detractors, even the more optimistic have argued that while the vector is moving in the right direction, the agreement reached was not enough, and adherence to even this low level of agreement is questionable, despite the urgency of the matter at hand.

In this case, it is likely that the private sector will be far more decisive and incisive than elected officials. In Glasgow, political leaders were criticized and key players such as China, India and Russia (representing nearly

---

[7] Sources: G7 UK Presidency 2021. Retrieved June 12, 2021; Research Institute – Global Wealth Databook 2018.

three billion people) did not show up. The hope and expectation of society is once again shifting to those who provide the capital and those who manage the capital, important levers for both shareholders and CEOs.

While governments should be responsible for setting the rules, lack of authority, fear for the next election, and the power of lobbyists, among other factors, make governments appear ineffective in addressing climate change. In the private sector, however, investors are under pressure from customers, regulators, and the public to use their power as shareholders to influence corporations' efforts to address climate change. Norway's sovereign wealth fund, one of the largest in the world with more than $1.2 trillion in assets and stakes in more than 9,000 companies in 70 countries, announced in September 2022 that its long-term returns will depend on how the companies it invests in manage the transition to zero emissions.[8] ABP, one of the world's largest pension funds, announced that it will divest 15 billion euros ($17.4 billion) in fossil fuel assets by early 2023.[9]

Some of the investors who remain as shareholders are willing to use more confrontational tactics – most notably, the successful campaign by an activist investor to join the board of ExxonMobil in 2021. Such activism is not only idealism and concern for the broader environment; it is also sound, risk-averse business. In 2021, BlackRock, the world's largest asset manager, predicted a cumulative loss in economic output of nearly 25 percent over the next two decades if no action is taken to mitigate climate change. Its research also predicts sharply reduced returns for sectors such as energy and utilities.

Investors, of course, recognize that they alone cannot change corporate behavior, so there is also a need for increased regulation and government policies to force companies to address emissions. But there is a growing recognition that the investment industry also has a role to play in the transition to a low-carbon economy, especially as demand for ESG investments grows. A recent survey of 6,000 individual investors in ten countries by NinetyOne, a UK-listed investment house, found that half of them believe asset managers should use their influence as shareholders to help drive emissions reductions in carbon-intensive companies.[10]

---

[8] WEF, Sep 23 2022, by Spencer Feingold.
[9] Bloomberg.com, by Alastair Marsh October 26, 2021.
[10] «Investors learn to exert pressure on heavy CO2 emitters», *Financial Times*, November, 2021.

The unification of Germany in 1990, for all its complexities, is probably the best example of a relatively recent equilibrium among the four estates, in which the leading constituent – the political system – was legitimized by the electorate as trustworthy and authoritative, and perceived as competent. The other three constituents stayed on the course within their own spheres of competence. The challenges of unification were daunting: economic, financial, social, political, psychological, and geopolitical. By comparison, the integration of two companies after a merger is widely regarded as a process with a high degree of entrepreneurial difficulty, due to cultural differences and modus operandi, meaning that the expected cost synergies and shareholder value creation can easily be derailed. The merger of two countries that had grown apart for forty years was unprecedented. It was a process that could have spun out of control on several fronts.

It did not. There was a clear vision, not necessarily shared by all, including the need to turn the page on the world wars, coupled with a new positioning for Europe and Germany as the Cold War was coming to an end. Key considerations included the conversion rate between West German and East German currencies and the size (and quality) of the debt that the unified Germany would inherit. It was decided to give priority to savings and East German pensions. In this scenario, the unknowns far outweighed the certainties: how to integrate a population accustomed to a socialist welfare state, how to restructure and sell off some 8,500 state-owned enterprise employing more than four million people, and how to make East Germans feel psychologically at home while de facto being overtaken by the West. Another focus was integrating a public administration and university system severely compromised by the Stasi (the repressive East German intelligence and secret police agency). Many European leaders had misgivings about the unification project, a sentiment best described by Italy's Prime Minister, Giulio Andreotti, who, quoting a maxim by François Mauriac, said: "We love Germany so much that we'd rather have two!"[11]

German reunification happened against all odds. In this particular historical moment, on the verge of the collapse of the Soviet Union and

---

[11] François Charles Mauriac was a French novelist, dramatist, critic, poet, and journalist, a member of the Académie française, and Nobel Prize laureate in Literature.

the Eastern bloc, roles were clear, leadership was earned, and competencies were synthesized by elected officials who, once they had absorbed the science and the technicalities of the case, provided leadership that businesses could follow.

For the most part, it was not difficult to maintain a collective narrative during this period of international construction. The media were primarily television, radio, and print, and in Europe they were all state-owned. The European media, including the BBC, were largely in tune with the political leadership and, by and large, worked in tandem with the policies set by elected officials. It was different in the United States. U.S. newspapers, in particular, became very critical in the 1970s, leading to two historic clashes between the government and the press that had fundamental implications for policy and trust.

In June 1971, the *New York Times* began publishing the "Pentagon Papers" in a series of news articles that summarized a forty-seven-volume secret government study of the origins of the Vietnam War. The study revealed no military secrets, but it was deeply politically disruptive. It uncovered government lies and policy disputes between America and South Vietnam. The White House tried to stop publication, but the Supreme Court ruled that the government had not proven its case that the Pentagon Papers were a threat to national security. Publication resumed, and the case severely damaged the U.S. government's ability to control information, as well as its credibility and reputation.

The Watergate scandal soon followed. Two *Washington Post* reporters, Bob Woodward and Carl Bernstein, broke the news of a wide range of illegal and unethical behavior directed by President Richard Nixon from the White House during his 1972 re-election campaign. These included disruption of Democratic Party campaign activities, burglary, and receipt of illegal campaign contributions. On August 9, 1974, Nixon became the first American president to resign from office.

Although Nixon was pardoned by his successor, Gerald Ford, the fact remained that the media had brought down a president. After a period of growth built on Western political harmony, hard-won international stability, and prosperity marked by visionary leadership, the bonds of trust began to erode. In many ways, this collapse of trust paralleled the rise of nongovernmental organizations, which today form a galaxy of charities, educational institutions, advocacy groups, and alliances with perspectives ranging from radical to conservative. Funding comes in from all sides, including individuals and governments, and goes out in myriad directions. When the World Bank and the IMF forced cuts in public services in the 1980s, NGOs stepped in to fill the gaps and have since become a global force.

There are, however, some positive signs of leadership by governments and institutions, such as the European Next Generation EU (NGEU) fund. Modeled after the Marshall Plan, it provides financial assistance to EU member states to help them recover from the adverse effects of the Covid-19 pandemic. The recovery plan totals €750 billion ($804 billion). At its heart is the €672.5 billion ($722 billion) Recovery and Resilience Facility, which is 46% grants and 54% loans. The aim is to support reforms and investments in each member state in the areas of labor markets, competition, fiscal discipline, public administration, and the judiciary.[12]

---

[12] Eucalls.net

3   The Present and Corporate Leadership

So far, we have looked at how the postwar structural equilibrium between the four estates of civil society – business, NGOs, the media, and government – was established. Beginning in the 1990s, this equilibrium changed, through a mix of deregulation, technological advances, the rise of business, the retrenchment of government, the rise of NGOs, and the expansion of the media.

Our current situation can be better understood by looking briefly at the economic drivers. The starting point was deregulation under Ronald Reagan in the United States. Prior to the Reagan presidency (1981-1989), the United States experienced a ten-year period of stagflation – high unemployment and high inflation. Reagan introduced lower marginal tax rates, simplified the income tax code, and continued deregulation.

This approach inspired British Prime Minister Margaret Thatcher. In 1986, the "Big Bang," the sudden deregulation of financial markets, included abolishing fixed commissions and eliminating the distinction between stockjobbers and stockbrokers on the London Stock Exchange. This encouraged liberalization in other financial markets, such as a similar Big Bang in Japan in the late 1990s. The effect on financial markets was dramatic leading to a global economic boom.

The 1990s became a "golden" decade, with the world mirroring the "globalization" levels of 1914.

3.1   The Ascent of Technology and Business

What is remarkable is the relative similarity in communications technology. The British economist John Maynard Keynes described life in 1914:

Figure 3.1 Capital Mobility in Modern History

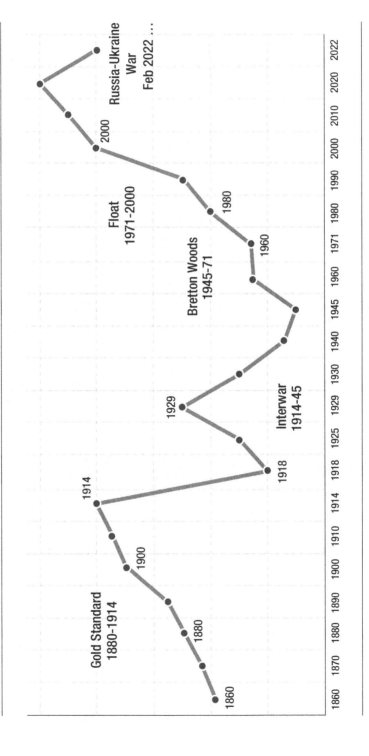

Source: Adapted from Globalization in historical perspective, Bordo, Taylor, Williamson

"When a man in London could travel the world freely, invest wherever he wanted, and could order by telephone, while sipping his morning tea in bed, the various products of the whole earth, in such quantity as he might see fit, and reasonably expect their early delivery upon his doorsteps."[1]

It is noteworthy that the Russian invasion of Ukraine means that the accompanying graph of capital mobility will have a downward curve. This marks the end of the holistic globalization as we have experienced it over the past thirty years, which was characterized by a decoupling of business from politics. Among other things, this permitted business activities with China, Russia and other non-democratic countries. The U.S. government, for example, wants now to source components and raw materials from "friendly" countries with shared values to increase the security of domestic production. While by no means perfect, it was characterized by prosperity, peace, and the rule of law, among other things. It was also a time of remarkable progress. Russia and Ukraine were integral parts of the global supply chain mosaic.

The war has severely disrupted global markets and exposed vulnerabilities in the security of raw material supplies – as illustrated below – critical to industrial production and the green transition (Fig. 3.2).

Figure 3.2 Ukraine Raw Material Supply

Raw Material	Industrial Application	Importance for green economy
Aluminum	Vehicles, airplanes, construction, power sector, food and beverage packaging	Battery casing and lightweight vehicle body parts for electric vehicles; electricity transmission lines, solar photovoltaic
Nickel	Stainless steel, magnets and alloys for construction, transport, medical equipment, electronic devices and power generation	Cathode materials for electric vehicles batteries
Palladium	Jewelry, dentistry, catalytic converters and in capacitors that store energy in electronic devices	Catalytic converters used to reduce emissions

(follows)

---

[1] *Economic Consequences of Peace*, J.M. Keynes, 1919.

(continues)

Potash	Plant and crop nutrient with quality-enhancing properties for fruit and vegetables, rice, wheat and other grains, sugar, corn, soybeans, palm oil and cotton	
Vanadium	Improves the stability and corrosion resistance of steel alloys for applications in space vehicles, nuclear reactors and airplanes. Some vanadium alloys used in superconducting magnets.	Vanadium redox flow batteries used in renewable energy storage; ongoing research into the use of vanadium in electric vehicle batteries

Source: OECD, *The supply of critical raw materials endangered by Russia's war on Ukraine*, 4 August 2022.

In 1990, the joys of today's technology and productivity were still a few years off. Internet connectivity was not widely available, broadband was still a concept, and mobile computers were big, heavy, and expensive, so they were shared in a pool. In Italy, where I lived, analog cell phones were just coming out, and the top model was the Motorola Dyna TAC 8800X. It was black, had a thin battery, and could fit in your pocket. That portability came at a price of about $4,000 – and it charged $1.00 per minute of talk time. It was exciting and liberating, and Europe became the world leader in mobile technology.

The European Public Telephone Operators (PTOs) banded together to form the Groupe Spéciale Mobile (GSM), which became the world standard for mobile phones, displacing competing U.S. systems. Nokia, a Finnish company, was the most innovative equipment manufacturer. In the mid-1990s, Italy's former national operator, Telecom Italia Mobile (TIM), introduced the prepaid mobile phone card, which was such an unexpected success that it made TIM the world's largest mobile operator.

Later, the U.S. low-earth-orbit cellular satellite constellations Iridium (backed by Motorola) and Globalstar (backed by Loral and Qualcomm) challenged European cell phone dominance by offering global mobile coverage. A Booz Allen Hamilton report warned Europe that to maintain this leadership, significant investment and the creation of major large-scale players would be critical to maintaining a winning position in a globalized world. Regrettably, today 5G mobile technology speaks primarily Chinese, with its corollary of national security concerns expressed on several continents.

Meanwhile, the second half of the 1990s saw the explosion of an entirely new phenomenon, the Internet. Over time, it precipitated a crisis in traditional "bricks-and-mortar" businesses, as the Internet could reach large segments of the population to deliver services or products without intermediaries.

Driven by the irresistible fascination of Silicon Valley, the Internet became the promised land, offering the opportunity to get rich very quickly. The traditional career value proposition of working hard for years to rise to the top and achieve financial wealth became the boring, dogged drudgery of the distant past. The gold rush was so pervasive that high-end professional services firms, such as banking and consulting were struggling to retain young employees, let alone hire new ones.

The late 1990s produced a hyper-egotistic cocktail, fueled by the self-confidence of technology that dwarfed traditional business giants in terms of capitalization, the availability of venture capital to conquer global markets, and the media's hunger for stories of smart kids whose Internet-based idea generated millions of dollars in funding by showing a business plan sketched on a napkin over a casual breakfast.

At the Charles Hotel, across the street from the Harvard Business School (HBS) campus in Cambridge, Massachusetts the world's leading employers hosted luxurious receptions for new graduates in an effort to recruit them. In the fall of 1997, this reception was deserted because it wasn't about the Internet. A fever had swept the U.S. and eventually Europe creating the dot-com bubble.

As trained analysts, my colleagues and I at Booz Allen Hamilton could not justify the staggering financial multiples of these startups. But there was a perception that the "old economy" was losing out to a newer parallel universe that would soon make everything else obsolete. Perception matters, especially in the Silicon Valley mindset. On Harvard's campus, a desperate high-end professional services firm, determined to hire talents, began delivering umbrellas with a *Have a nice day!* card to the dorm rooms of the students they wanted to target.

And the crash did come about. Between 1995 and March 2000 (at its peak), the Nasdaq Composite stock market index rose 400%, only to fall 78% from its peak by October 2002, wiping out all the gains made during the bubble. While investment in startups recovered, it never returned to the folly of those years.

Another aspect of the Internet's appeal was that it was more or less unregulated. The launch of GBDe (Global Business Dialogues on e-commerce) in New York in January 1999 was a critical step in the company's ascent.[2] GBDe, one of the first global business groups to organize itself around public policy issues, represented the global cooperation of companies from around the world and served as a prototype for future business-government interaction. Corporations were taking on a number of challenges facing e-commerce,[3] and GBDe emerged as the de facto private authority in the global public policy debate on the topic, declaring, *"Governments around the world should recognize the dangers that regulation of the Internet would pose to their economies and societies."*[4] GBDe asserted the primacy of the private sector over elected government officials. As Time Warner CEO Gerald Levin stated in a press session following the New York meeting: *"We have a role to play in the shaping of public policy, and we are truly capable of rising above ... narrow geographic issues."*[5]

The business world was pushing hard towards liberalization, globalization and transnational operations. The rise of business was accompanied by a series of events. In 1989, the fall of communism; in 1990, the reunification of Germany; in 1991, the collapse of the Soviet Union; in 1997, the U.S. Taxpayer Relief Act, which lowered the top marginal tax rate on capital gains, making business more attractive for speculative investment; in 2001, China's entry into the WTO[6]; and in 2002, the introduction of the single European currency, the euro. Most importantly, as noted above, this expansion has been peaceful and in accordance with international law. A wave of breakthrough technologies and a wave of privatization and liberalization all contributed to building optimism and an unshakable belief in the future. All in the name of business.

---

[2] Inspired by EU Commissioner Martin Bangemann in a 1997 speech at the Telecom Interactive '97 conference, Geneva, Switzerland; "governments, regulators, and industry to work together to establish a new global framework for communications for the next millennium".

[3] Issue groups in 1999 (Corporation leading): Consumer Confidence (Daimler Chrysler), Content/Commercial Communication (Walt Disney), Liability (Telefonica), Authentication/security (NEC), Jurisdiction (EDS), Tax & Tariffs (Deutsche Bank), Information Infrastructure (Nortel NW), Protection of Personal Data (Toshiba), IP rights (Fujitsu).

[4] GBDe 1999 New York, CEOs declaration.

[5] See "The Global Business Dialogue on e-commerce (GBDe): Private Firms, Public Policy, Global Governance" by Maria Green Cowles, School of International Service, American University.

[6] China joined the World Trade Organization on December 11, 2001.

Today, this balancing act is much more difficult than it used to be. One factor is the extraordinary speed and complexity of recent globalization. Unprecedented disruptive technologies are another. Covid-19 remains a problem, but the vaccine seems to have halted the lethality of the virus, at least for now. The war between Russia and Ukraine has added more unknowns to an already complicated equation. While Western leaders were focused on managing a post-Covid environment and considering what the "new normal" paradigm would be, the invasion of Ukraine has caused rising inflation and interest rates, lower consumer confidence, possible stagnation, forced redesign of value chains, recession, and the potential for significant unemployment.

These disruptions have put a limit on the illusory idea of a one-click utopia, ever easier and app-driven for personal avatars, remote from the effects of society. At the same time, these technologies have been essential to the millions of employees who have learned how to work remotely, leading to an unprecedented change in workplace norms. We have yet to discern the matrix of the "new normal" and help shape it for the benefit of all. For many, remote work has improved quality of life and work-life balance. On the other hand, the "office" has always supported aspects such as team spirit and camaraderie that are essential to organizational cohesion and productivity, elements that are much harder to build in a virtual world. This is even more true for the younger generation, the digital natives, who have spent the last years of their education in the virtual world. They search for and need communal identity, within which work identity is a major component. CEOs from all industries must work together with government to bring to fruition this extraordinary new phase of human society, even to the extent that innovative work-related legislation may be entailed.

3.2   The Retrenchment of Governments

Over the past three decades, the success of the business value proposition and the resulting competition to attract the best and the brightest young talents has sometimes come at the expense of the public sector. This trend continues today.

And while consumers have benefited from the simplicity of using services through the vast array of apps available on smartphones, the enabling world behind the scenes is far from simple. It is technology-centered and capital intensive, based on sophisticated value chains that span continents. This complexity makes it difficult to understand, and even more difficult to govern. Joshua McCrain, in his paper *Human Capital on Capitol Hill*, identifies the challenges of this complexity for lawmakers:

> *Policymaking in Congress is complex and only getting more difficult as members must increasingly rely on their own staff for technical aspects of legislating…, leaving rank-and-file members more reliant on their own offices to gather information about policy and voting…. In other words, the ability of rank-and-file members to be productive legislators hinges largely on their own initiative and staff.*[7]

This feeds into the public-private relationship as a product of recent decades. As corporations became global and financially powerful, parliaments were somewhat marginalized by the epochal changes affecting local constituencies, and the jobs of elected officials in Western democracies began to be perceived as a cost to be bear. The rise of offshoring and smart sourcing practices favored China and Asia and increasingly affected the Western workforce: engineering graduates, for example, struggled to find jobs in the US as employers found lower-cost workers in Asia. Policymakers have long lacked an understanding of the dynamics that globalization was introducing into Western economies, from the labor market to the redistribution of wealth and its impact on inequality. This growing inability to mediate between the needs of capital and the well-being of the population at large was marked by an abdication of policymaking.

At a dinner with Silicon Valley's top luminaries in January 2012, President Barack Obama asked Steve Jobs what it would take to make iPhones in the United States. According to the *New York Times*, in 2011 "almost all of the 70 million iPhones, 30 million iPads and 59 million other products Apple sold were manufactured overseas." Jobs dryly replied, "Those jobs aren't coming back."[8]

---

[7] *Human Capital on Capitol Hill*, April 9, 2021, Joshua McCrain, Post-doctoral Research Associate, Michigan State University, https://joshuamccrain.com/wp-content/uploads/2021/04/McCrain-Human-Capital.pdf

[8] *New York Times*, January 21, 2012, Charles Duhigg and Keith Bradsher.

In the face of diminishing government influence, voter turnout has been declining around the world since the early 1990s as the political system struggles to provide holistic solutions for ordinary people. This trend in democratic participation has raised many concerns. Fewer citizens see elections as the main tool for legitimizing the control of political parties over policymaking. However, lower voter turnout does not necessarily mean that citizens are becoming less politically active. On the contrary, we have seen an increase in other forms of citizen activism, such as mass protests, occupy movements, and the proliferation of social media used as a new platform for political engagement.[9]

3.3   NGOs

The void left by the political system was filled by non-governmental organizations. It was during this period that NGOs gained credibility, and trust, because:[10]

- They were always on the offensive.
- They took their message to the consumer.
- They were adept at building coalitions.
- They always had a clear agenda.
- They moved at Internet speed.
- They spoke the language of the media.

There was a strong perception that the spirit of NGOs was a mission to selflessly serve the greater good, especially on social issues where politics had abdicated. A further boost to the popularity of NGOs came when the United Nations began to distinguish between intergovernmental organizations (IGO or IO) and private organizations. IGOs are formed when governments enter into an agreement, such as the United Nations, the World Trade Organization, or NATO. By allowing the private sector to operate as non-profit NGOs, this constituency was able to channel an infinite number of causes and funding.

---

[9] Voter Turnout Trends around the World, by Abdurashid Solijonov; 2016 International Institute for Democracy and Electoral Assistance.

[10] 2021 Edelman Trust Barometer.

The NGO sector is now one of the world's largest employers, worth more than $1 trillion annually and employing more than 19 million paid staff and countless volunteers.[11] The Bill and Melinda Gates Foundation is one of the most prominent and active, with the world's largest endowment of $28.8 billion. Another major NGO is the Clinton Global Initiative (CGI), founded in 2005 by former President Bill Clinton. It represented the most advanced model of cross-sector collaboration, projects in which corporations, NGOs, and governments work together to address a specific problem. The CGI "gathered global and emerging leaders to create and implement solutions to the world's most pressing challenges."

One of my New York partners and co-author of *Megacommunities* was a key supporter of the Clintons, helping them to establish the Clinton Foundation in Harlem.[12] He introduced me to CGI's September meetings in New York, where the guest speakers included eminent heads of state, the world's most prominent CEOs, and a number of Hollywood stars who were commendably committed to making a difference. Participants were asked to join forces in a spirit of cross-sector cooperation. The formula was innovative, pragmatic and engaging, and President Clinton's charisma naturally played a key role. Progress was monitored by the CGI team over the subsequent year.

When necessary, President Clinton personally attended meetings around the world. Each year, the former president presented awards to teams that had achieved concrete results since the prior meeting.

Topics included the fight against poverty, HIV/AIDS, and climate change. One of the most intriguing collaborations involved the Israeli-Palestinian conflict. A team from each side would work to create jobs for Palestinians in an effort to heal decades-old wounds. CGI was a breath of fresh air that finally made global problems seem manageable. President Clinton embodied the facilitator of positive change for the greater good. As a former politician, he had the network of relation-

---

[11] GFP. From The 21st Century NGO: In the Market for Change by Sustainability in partnership with the United Nations and several other organizations and corporations. This study reveals that many NGOs are now shifting from their traditional confrontational roles to more collaborative interactions with governments and businesses. See http://www.sustainability.com/insight/research-article.asp?id=51

[12] Reginald (Reggie) Van Lee.

ships, the experience and, through his leadership of this organization, the speed of execution. In 2016, the prospect of a conflict of interest should Hillary Clinton be elected president forced CGI to close, but it returned in 2022.

The success of these organizations contributed to a growing perception that governments were no longer capable of leading and solving critical problems. Today, NGOs that need to raise money to fund their projects act and are organized like businesses. There was a period of confusion as they seemed to lose the magic of perceived selflessness, beginning to seem accountable to financiers more than stakeholders.

3.4 The Media

Over the same period, the rise of the Internet posed a serious challenge to traditional media. A relatively small field of television and radio stations and newspapers was once the most reliable and sought-after source of information. Largely considered independent of overt political leanings, these outlets had the trust of their large audiences, and the credibility and prestige to mediate opinion as the guardians of a relatively measured political and civic discourse.

The Internet revolutionized and fragmented this orderly world. It turns each individual into a source of à la carte information, losing quality and reliability, while having to become increasingly sensational to attract traffic. This competition feeds the wildest spirits, at the expense of truth and ethics. The 72% trust mark achieved by traditional media in the post-Watergate era was long lost by the start of the new millennium. Financially, the combination of technology and money accumulated by the Web giants started to divert advertising from traditional media. The challenge of this constituent is best described by Richard Haass: "social media is especially pernicious, as it tends to undermine social trust, weaken institutions, create mini societies with their own narratives [...] many gravitate to outlets that reflect not just their interests but their biases. Missing is any quality control. [...] Misinformation is rampant, balance rarely found."[13]

---

[13] Richard Haass, *The Bill of Obligations. The Ten Habits of Good Citizens*, Penguin Press, 2023.

Despite many efforts, including the Trust Project – an international consortium devoted to making journalism more transparent – media credibility and trust have plummeted.[14] According to Edelman's 2023 assessment, 42% of respondents in 25 countries view the media as a source of misleading information. In 2023, trust in the media has declined in 16 countries since 2022.[15]

Figure 3.3   Trust in Media in Countries under 50% Trust, 2023

Country	Trust in Media	Change 2022 to 2023
Germany	47	0
Italy	47	-3
Brazil	46	-1
USA	43	+4
South Africa	41	0
Sweden	41	NA
Ireland	40	-5
France	39	+1
Argentina	38	-5
Australia	38	-5
Colombia	38	0
Spain	38	-2
UK	37	+2
Japan	34	-1
South Korea	27	-6

Legend: 60-100 Trust; 50-59 Neutral; 1-49 Distrust

Source: Adapted by the author from 2023 Edelman Trust Barometer

The political polarizations that occurred in all major democracies exacerbated differences and, in turn, strained these societies by accentuating the magnitude of a range of problems. Meanwhile, a frenetic and vicious media cycle encourages political recourse to easy and often temporary patchwork solutions.

The fragmentation of the media landscape and its consumption has led to an erosion of trust in the media. Information overload and instant access have fundamentally changed consumption patterns and expecta-

---

[14] https://thetrustproject.org/
[15] 2023 Edelman Trust Barometer.

tions. The spiral of "doomscrolling" addiction, anxiety, and misinformation has proven very difficult to stop. The quality and reliability so essential to media and news are not necessarily valued by the end consumer.

We have encountered testing times before. On September 11, 2001, Booz Allen Hamilton's global partners were meeting in New York City when the Twin Towers were struck by terrorists. Although I was a partner and managing director for Italy at the time, I had to stay in Milan that day for a presentation to a client's board of directors instead of attending the meeting in New York. No one from Booz Allen Hamilton was injured in that city, but tragically, three colleagues who were briefing a client at the Pentagon outside of Washington, DC, were killed when the hijacked passenger jet crashed into that military facility. The memories and emotions of those hours, when communication between colleagues was nearly impossible, are still very much with me. These attacks changed the world, including the perception of a "flat world" that could be conquered with a clever business plan.

The October 25, 2001 issue of *The Economist* carried the headline "How the world has (and hasn't) changed." While the trajectory of globalization proved to be resilient, the gap between business and government widened as each focused on its core function. The economic recession, a risk even before September 11, accelerated. In response, governments adopted compensatory monetary and fiscal policies to boost demand. The eight-month "dot-bomb" recession from March to November 2001 was followed by the eighteen-month "Great Recession" from December 2007 to June 2009, the worst economic downturn since the recession of 1937-38. Finally, Covid-19 caused a two-month recession from February to April 2020.

So, our societies are resilient and can evolve. However, the IMF[16] said in a blog post on May 22, 2022 that the global economy is facing its "biggest test since World War II." Combining the Russia-Ukraine war, the Covid-19 pandemic, increased financial market volatility, and the ongoing threat of climate change, the IMF said the world faces a "potential confluence of calamities."[17] This is of a different and urgent magnitude. In this context, companies are aware of and concerned about the need to restore some kind of balance between the four estates, and especially between government and business. Chapter VI will explain why the IRG methodology is effective, timely, and necessary in this effort.

---

[16] By IMF Managing Director Kristalina Georgieva.
[17] CNBC.com, May 23, 2022 by Elliot Smith.

3.5   The Proactive Corporation and the Cost of Blindness

Stakeholder expectations have become limitless. In the absence of polit-ical vision and mediation, companies can be dragged into politics. Some have been proactive and good listeners, responding to rising expectations. Others continued to view a growing issue as out of scope and therefore irrelevant to their core business. JP Morgan is a good example of the former, while Delta and Coca Cola are the latter.

JP Morgan, Berkshire Hathaway, and Amazon formed their own health care provider networks and tried to solve the conundrum that con-tinues to confound lawmakers: reliable service at affordable prices. Ad-vancing the Black Pathways initiative, JP Morgan Chase announced in 2019 that it aims to reduce the wealth gap in jobs and prosperity for Black Americans through a bold $30 billion commitment to advance racial eq-uity and create economic opportunity for Black and Latino communities between 2019 and 2023. Advancing Cities is another example of filling the gap left by the political system. It is a $500 million, five-year initia-tive to invest in solutions that strengthen the long-term vitality of the world's cities and the communities within them that have not benefited from economic growth.[18]

In 2021, Delta and Coca-Cola, both of which are based in Atlan-ta, faced the threat of boycotts from activists who said these companies needed to do more to oppose new limits on voting in the state of Georgia. Both companies called the law unacceptable. Dozens of Black executives, including Merck & Co CEO Kenneth Frazier, called on their peers in corporate America to push back against broader voting restrictions.[19] In-terestingly, Delta's criticism was a reactive course reversal for the airline, which had expressed neutral ambivalence in a statement a week earlier. "American companies need to take a stand," Kenneth Chenault, former CEO of American Express, told Reuters. "We're calling on corporate America to publicly oppose any discriminatory legislation and all mea-sures designed to limit Americans' ability to vote." A letter supporting Frazier and Chenault's campaign was signed by 72 Black executives, in-cluding former Xerox CEO Ursula Burns, former Citigroup Chairman Richard Parsons, and Uber Chief Legal Officer, Tony West.

---

[18] https://www.jpmorganchase.com/impact/communities/advancingcities
[19] Reuters, March 31, 2021.

Such examples show us that committed action across the corporate sector can have a fundamentally positive impact on the sustainable quality of human society and prosperity. Managed correctly, it will yield a corresponding corporate prosperity. Mismanaged or ignored, the consequences can sometimes be severe and come from unexpected sources. The lack of sensors to gauge how society is turning and evolving comes at a price, especially in an era of the instant communication of mass sentiment and global connectivity. Today, in addition to such concerns, the world faces costs of a different scale and consequences that cannot be eliminated by paying fines.

It is clear from what we have described so far that we are approaching a *changement d'époque*, a "change of era."

This is of a different order of magnitude from an *époque de changement*, an era of change such as the 1990s, when a series of breakthrough technologies transformed the way we live and work. For all the dynamism of this technological change, it occurred against a backdrop of seemingly endless continuity. A *changement d'époque*, on the other hand, represents a rupture with the past and the beginning of a new era to which companies must adapt.

4 The Early Stages: Corporate Social Responsibility (CSR)

Corporate Social Responsibility (CSR) has come a long way from being a nice thing to do to what it is today: a necessity for a successful business.

Today's CSR programs have their roots in corporate philanthropy, an early attempt by companies to consider the well-being not only of shareholders and direct stakeholders, but also of employees and then society as a whole. In the mid-to-late 1800s, there was growing concern about the well-being of workers and their working conditions. Andrew Carnegie donated large portions of his wealth to educational causes and scientific research; John D. Rockefeller, who made his fortune in the oil industry, followed Carnegie's lead and donated more than half a billion dollars to religious, educational, and scientific causes.

These businessmen understood that the role of corporations could be more than just doing business and could contribute to the well-being of society where governments were unable to play a decisive role.

Social activist groups (and others) advocated corporate social responsibility throughout the 1950s and '60s. The term itself was coined in 1953 by Howard Bowen, an American economist, in his publication *Social Responsibilities of the Businessman*.

CSR became popular in the U.S. in the 1970's, when the Committee for Economic Development proposed the concept of a "social contract" between business and society. The social contract is based on a simple idea: business functions because of public "consent," therefore business has an obligation to constructively serve the needs of society, in a sort of *do ut des* can be seen as a "license to operate" – that is, to contribute more to society than just their commercial products.

In 1985, Archie B. Carroll, a professor of management at the University of Georgia, in *The Evolution of the Corporate Social Performance Model*, proposed a definition of CSR as a three-pronged approach:

1. companies adopt principles (or ethics),
2. created and implement formal processes (how they respond),
3. and develop policies (managing specific issues).

Carroll's approach brought together social responsiveness and business ethics into a single field of study and performance, and in 1991 he created a graphic depiction of CSR with the publication of the book *The Pyramid of Corporate Social Responsibility*. Carroll was able to take this nuanced topic and simplify the concept of CSR with a single pyramid diagram, making the model the new mainstream business approach.

Carroll chose a pyramid because it is a simple design that easily illustrates how a company has four types of responsibilities:

1. to be economically profitable,
2. to obey the law,
3. to be ethically responsible,
4. to give to philanthropic causes.

Many other practitioners, such as economist Theodore Levitt, criticized the new mainstream theory of corporate social responsibility on the grounds that the long-term goal of business is profit maximization. Building on Levitt's arguments, the Nobel Prize-winning economist Milton Friedman also argued that social issues aren't the concern of business, and that social problems will be solved through the unfettered operation of the free market.

Such opposition has led to the presentation of CSR in terms of a business case – that is, how does CSR benefit business?

From a business perspective, Johnson & Johnson, whose founder, Robert Wood Johnson, established its credo in 1943, was one of the earliest adopters of CSR. Several CSR initiatives took place in the first half of the last century, and its founders understood that their stakeholders extended beyond the board room. What's more, if their customers and communities were healthy and vibrant, so too would their businesses be.

Today, CSR is essential to the bottom line, and corporate citizenship professionals are empowered to align their work with the business to maximize its impact. Public authorities, including the EU, also have an important role to play in supporting and encouraging companies to act responsibly. Over the years, voluntary and mandatory measures to promote CSR and Responsible Business Conduct (RBC) have been developed, implementing the UN Guiding Principles on Business and Human Rights (UNGPs) and the UN 2030 Agenda for Sustainable Development[1].

---

[1] https://www.un.org/sustainabledevelopment/

5 The Current ESG Metrics: Introduction, Rise, Evolution and Limits

ESG, which stands for Environmental, Social, and Governance, is a framework for assessing the sustainability and ethics of a company's practices, investments or – more broadly – business activities. The term is now commonly used to emphasize companies' adherence to a set of rules and behaviors that reflect greater attention to transparency in governance and respect for the outside world. The concept has evolved over time, as have societal values and concerns about corporate behavior and responsibility.

The practice of ESG investing began in the 1960s as socially responsible investing, where investors excluded stocks or entire industries from their portfolios based on business activities such as tobacco production or dealings with the South African apartheid regime. Today, ESG has become a key driver of new metrics that analyze a company's risks, opportunities, and qualities.

As Larry Fink of BlackRock has stated:

> *"The public expectations of your company have never been greater. Society is demanding that companies, both public and private, serve a social purpose. To prosper over time, every company must not only deliver financial performance, but also show how it makes a positive contribution to society. Companies must benefit all of their stakeholders, including shareholders, employees, customers, and the communities in which they operate."*[1]

---

[1] *A Sense of Purpose*, posted by Larry Fink, BlackRock, Inc., on Wednesday, January 17, 2018, https://corpgov.law.harvard.edu/2018/01/17/a-sense-of-purpose/

5.1   An Introduction to ESG Letter by Letter

E - The environmental component of ESG has its roots in the environmental movement of the 1960s and 1970s, which brought attention to the negative effect of industrial activities on the environment. More recently, this attention has led firms to analyze the environmental impact of their own operations and value chain, such as climate change or biodiversity, and to work to reduce their negative footprint. These factors have become vital to consider; in fact, an overall positive environmental impact helps to reduce business risks related to environmental issues and aims to ensure business sustainability in the long term.

S - The social component of ESG emerged somewhat later, much more in the 1980s and especially in the 1990s, as investors and companies became increasingly aware of the impact that corporate behavior can have on society. In general, the core elements are equality, human rights, ethics, and inclusion – factors that address a company's relationship with different groups of people, such as employees, stakeholders, and society. The criteria for analysis can range from fair pay for employees of different genders to fair treatment of customers and suppliers, as well as support for initiatives to address poor working conditions, especially in subsidiaries, affiliated companies or the supply chain. In recent years, social factors have become particularly relevant, especially those related to diversity, inclusion and gender equality.

G - The governance component of ESG emerged in the early 2000s, following the dot-com bubble and a series of corporate scandals and governance failures such as Enron and Parmalat. This factor focuses on how a company operates internally, applying (or not applying) corporate policies, internal controls and practices to comply with regulations and best practices. Governance focuses on the composition of the company's management and board, ensuring that the structure is diverse and inclusive, particularly in terms of skills and backgrounds, as well as business integrity and transparency. In promoting new governance plans, companies are now considering, for example, financial reporting standards or whistleblowing programs and ethical business practices to implement anti-corruption and anti-bribery policies.

5.2 What Are the ESG Factors?

One step further, ESG has overtaken CSR in mainstream thinking, consolidating its role as a possible business response to societal needs.

This has probably happened because ESG factors have been studied in a much more "valuable" way by the academic world, which has developed ESG indicators and ratings that allow measurability and comparability of company performance in ESG-related areas. MSCI, an ESG pioneer which launched the world's first socially responsible index in 1990, affirms, "The *ESG rating is designed to measure a company's resilience to long-term, industry material environmental, social and governance (ESG) risks.*"[2]

The primary purpose of the factors is to evaluate practices, policies, and initiatives in all three dimensions of ESG: Environmental, Social and Governance.

For the first dimension, Environmental, the focus is on climate change, natural resources, pollution and waste, and environmental opportunities.

For the second dimension, Social, the focus is on human capital, product liability, stakeholder opposition, and social opportunities.

The third dimension, Governance, centers on corporate governance and corporate behavior.

5.2.1 *ESG Environmental Factors*

MSCI classifies the following factors as Environmental Key Issues when conducting its own ESG research:

Climate change:

- carbon emissions, which measures the amount of greenhouse gas emissions a company emits directly, through its own operations, or indirectly via its value chain;
- product carbon footprint, i.e. the total greenhouse gas emissions generated by a product throughout its lifecycle, from raw material extraction to end-of-life. Depending on whether the company

---

[2] https://www.msci.com/esg-101-what-is-esg/evolution-of-esg-investing

is business-to-business (B2B) or business-to-consumer (B2C), the product footprint may have a different scope:

- – Cradle-to-gate: quantifies the total greenhouse gas emissions from raw material extraction to product manufacturing for manufacturers, or distribution and retail for retailers. This type of measurement is used for B2B products,
- – Cradle-to-grave: considers the total greenhouse gas emissions generated during the entire life cycle of the product, i.e. from the raw material extraction to product manufacturing, distribution, use, disposal, and possible recycling. This form is used for B2C;

• financing environmental impact, which analyzes the environmental risk associated with the lending and underwriting activities of financial institutions;

• climate change vulnerability, which assesses a company's exposure to extreme climate events. In particular, this parameter considers how exposed a company's own operations and supply chain are to climate change, as well as the countries in which the company is located.

Natural resources:

• water stress, which quantifies the water intensity of a company's own operations as well as the company's efforts to manage water-related risks and opportunities;

• biodiversity and land use, which considers a firm's efforts to minimize the impact of its own operations on biodiversity and to manage land use carefully;

• raw materials sourcing, which assesses the sustainability of a company's supply chain in terms of its traceability and certification, and analyzes the impact of the raw materials used on the planet.

Pollution and waste:

• toxic emissions and waste, which measures the toxic or carcinogenic emission that may result from a company's own operations and its efforts to minimize the associated damage to the planet;

• packaging and waste, which focuses on a company's mix of packaging materials, and the efforts to minimize their environmental impact – for example, implementing waste management policies and educating consumers about recycling through labeling;

- electronic waste, which looks at a company's electronic waste production and recycling efforts – for example, considering the amount of electronic waste produced and the facilities used to collect and recycle it.

Environmental opportunities:

- clean technology opportunities, which analyzes the company's commitment to innovative clean technologies – for example, considering its R&D spending, its strategic investments in this area, and the revenues associated with the adoption of clean technologies;
- green building opportunities, which considers the carbon footprint of a company's properties, its exposure to green building regulations, such as the certification of its green commitment to the country's regulatory standards, and the company's efforts to improve the environmental performance of its real estate assets;
- renewable energy opportunities, which evaluates the company's efforts to develop renewable energy generation capacity.

5.2.2 *ESG Social Factors*

Social factors may not be as easy to measure as environmental factors.

Recently, however, people have begun to pay special attention to these issues, prompting companies to implement new initiatives and reporting standards to demonstrate their commitment to the cause. Key drivers have been stakeholder expectations and, in some cases, regulatory requirements such as workplace health and safety standards or minimum wage.

In its own ESG Research, MSCI has identified the following factors as Social Key Issues:

Human capital:

- Labour management, which evaluates a company's workforce in terms of its composition, size, and diversity, as well as the relationship between management and employees. Also included here is the level of employee engagement, various forms of compensation (including nonwage benefits), and the measures taken to ensure worker safety and protection.

- Human capital development, which analyses a company's ability to attract, train and retain talented, skilled employees. Elements such as employee ownership, feedback processes, leadership training offered, and talent development pipelines are used to measure this factor.
- Health and safety, which examines a company's workplace and its compliance with health and safety standards/regulations.
- Supply chain labour standards, including the level of transparency and traceability and the efforts to ensure fair working conditions.

Product liability:

- Product safety and quality, which measures a company's exposure to potential product safety complaints; the quality of its supply chain, from sourcing to manufacturing processes (supplier training, quality controls, product testing); and correct marketing practices.
- Chemical safety, which assesses the potential presence of hazardous chemicals in a company's product and its efforts to find alternatives. It also considers a company's exposure to new or more stringent chemical regulations.
- Financial product safety, which looks at financial institutions and their potential exposure to unethical financial lending or the mis-selling of financial products to customers.
- Privacy and data security, which evaluates the amount of personal data a company collects and its exposure to potential new or stricter privacy regulations, as well as the strength of the systems developed to protect the data and the risk of data breaches.
- Responsible investment, which measures the extent to which environmental, social, and governance factors are integrated in a company's own assets or those it invests in on behalf of third parties. This can be analyzed by considering the level of disclosure on ESG matters, the number of employees dedicated to ESG issues, the commitment to sustainable initiatives, and the level of ESG considerations in the investment process.
- Health and demographic risk, which primarily concerns insurance companies and their ability to manage emerging social risks and to create and develop new insurance products to address new health or social trends.

Stakeholder opposition:

- Controversial sourcing, which evaluates a company's reliance on raw materials imported from conflict zones and its efforts to ensure traceability and certification of the sourcing process.

Social opportunities:

- Access to communications, which evaluates a company's efforts to provide information and expand networks in underserved areas of the world.
- Access to finance, which assesses a company's attempts to extend financial services to underserved markets, such as small businesses, and to adopt innovative distribution channels.
- Access to healthcare, which considers a company's efforts to ensure access to healthcare services and products in developing countries, through fair pricing mechanisms and engagement in social initiatives.
- Health and nutrition opportunities, which evaluates the quality of nutritional values in a company's products and its endeavors to make products healthier.

5.2.3 *ESG Governance Factors*

MSCI classifies the following factors as Governance Key Issues when conducting its own ESG research:

Corporate governance:

- Board diversity, which evaluates the quality of a company's board of directors using inclusion and diversity parameters – for example, how many women are in executive positions.
- Executive compensation, which analyzes the salary of the CEO and other members of the executive team and compares them to their peers.
- Ownership and control, which assesses a company's ownership structure and control bias (the ratio of economic and voting power held by the largest shareholder), as well as other ownership elements that may augment governance risk.

- Accounting, which refers to a company's potential accounting risk, as assessed by the external audit process (firm selection, audit report findings).

Corporate behavior:

- Business ethics, which evaluates a company's practices for dealing with ethical business issues such as management misconduct, corruption, bribery, money laundering, and fraud.
- Anti-competitive practices, which evaluates a company's efforts to promote proper standards of competition and enforce antitrust regulations.
- Tax transparency, which examines a company's estimated tax gap – the difference between the effective corporate tax rate and the statutory tax rate – and any other potential involvement in tax-related controversies.
- Corruption and instability, which considers how a company reviews and attempts to mitigate corruption risks along its value chain.
- Financial system instability, which assesses a company's exposure to potential financial instability in the marketplace and its efforts to mitigate this risk.

The whole ESG framework can easily be wrapped up in the following figure by MSCI.

5.3   ESG Ratings

Over the past decade, the ESG ratings have grown exponentially as interest in the topic from a social perspective has increased. According to KPMG, *"At the same time ESG ratings have become important when investors analyze their potential future investments, and therefore it should not be neglected by companies."*

The goal of ESG ratings is to measure a company's exposure to risks and opportunities related to environmental, social and governance topics. Undoubtedly investors prefer to invest in companies with a good rating, as these businesses often have easier access to capital in the credit markets, can build a better brand reputation, can attract talent, and should have greater control over various risks.

Figure 5.1 Esg Key Issues Framework

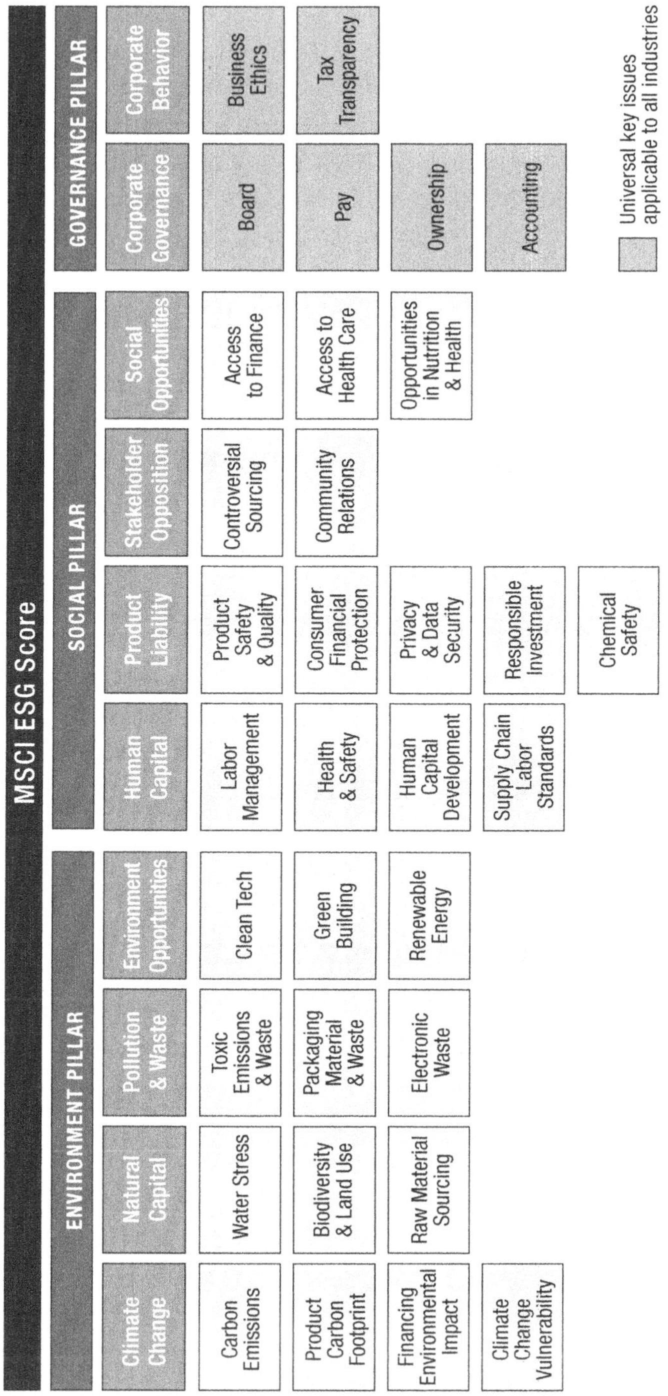

MSCI ESG Score

ENVIRONMENT PILLAR				SOCIAL PILLAR				GOVERNANCE PILLAR	
Climate Change	Natural Capital	Pollution & Waste	Environment Opportunities	Human Capital	Product Liability	Stakeholder Opposition	Social Opportunities	Corporate Governance	Corporate Behavior
Carbon Emissions	Water Stress	Toxic Emissions & Waste	Clean Tech	Labor Management	Product Safety & Quality	Controversial Sourcing	Access to Finance	Board	Business Ethics
Product Carbon Footprint	Biodiversity & Land Use	Packaging Material & Waste	Green Building	Health & Safety	Consumer Financial Protection	Community Relations	Access to Health Care	Pay	Tax Transparency
Financing Environmental Impact	Raw Material Sourcing	Electronic Waste	Renewable Energy	Human Capital Development	Privacy & Data Security		Opportunities in Nutrition & Health	Ownership	
Climate Change Vulnerability				Supply Chain Labor Standards	Responsible Investment			Accounting	
					Chemical Safety				

☐ Universal key issues applicable to all industries

Source: MSCI Website

But because the rating model is open to study and discovery, companies can improve their ratings by analyzing the rating agencies' methodologies and the results of their analyses, and by understanding the meaning of each criterion and where the company's strengths and weaknesses lie. Ratings are often driven by a lack of data and reporting, but they can also be driven by ESG strategy and whether the reporting meets market expectations.

The question is whether ratings have become popular to meet the needs of the public or the needs of companies to comply with the new rules of the market.

It's clear that ESG ratings have evolved over time in order to analyze and measure a company's management of financially relevant ESG risks and opportunities. That's why today, in the words of Silda Wall Spitzer and John Mandyck (2019)[3], *"every listed company board must now become 'sustainability fluent."*

Given the growing relevance of sustainability in the business world, measuring ESG factors and determining ESG scores has become increasingly important. According to Spitzer and Mandyck, the general process of creating ESG scores is divided into three phases:

a. Disclosure platforms. First, companies must disclose their sustainability-related information. This is critical because there is no single framework for ESG ratings, as there is for accounting practices. This means comparisons between companies that use different disclosure standards can be extremely complex.
b. Rating agencies. These are third-party firms that collect the sustainability information disclosed by companies and, after performing a series of analyses, assign them an ESG score/rating. Probably the most widely used and highly regarded rating company is MSCI. Note that rating agencies do not need permission from companies to conduct their analyses.
c. Rating reporting. Finally, rating agencies sell the newly calculated ESG scores to interested data providers such as Bloomberg or Yahoo.

---

[3] Wall Spitzer S., Mandyck J., «What Boards Need to Know About Sustainability Ratings», *Harvard Business Review*, 2019.

Why calculate ESG scores?

Given the growing attention to ESG issues, companies need a way to objectively assess their ESG performance, which measures their commitment and ability to manage ESG risks and opportunities.

Are these scores really useful for understanding the quality of a company's governance, its risks and opportunities, its compliance with various standards, and its overall sustainability over the long term? This question can easily be turned into another one: "Are these scores able to capture at a glance companies' responses to society's expressed and unexpressed needs?"

Assessing a company's ESG effort has become a fundamental part of the investment process. Investors today are looking for "green" companies to diversify their portfolios and financial risk, and to feel better about themselves.

Once a company has analyzed and evaluated its ESG performance, the next logical step is to communicate these measures in a consistent and clear manner. Indeed, ESG reporting has a number of benefits for the company, such as building a good reputation and attracting conscientious investors. Moreover, sustainability reporting is now considered as important as financial reporting. This is evidenced by the fact that the number of rules and regulations on the subject has grown exponentially in recent years. Finally, setting clear rules for the disclosure of ESG information is critical to avoid greenwashing – misleading the market by lying about a company's true commitment to environmental best practices.

Over the past few decades, a large number of accounting frameworks and standards have emerged to define consistent ways to disclose and report ESG data. But by 2022, the majority of ESG reporting will come from voluntary disclosure. According to a research report published in November 2022 by Governance & Accountability Institute, 96% of companies in the S&P 500 and 81% of companies in the Russell 1000 published sustainability reports in 2021.[4]

In recent years, supranational bodies such as the European Parliament have also produced a number of regulations that attempt to set rules for European companies to follow with regard to the transparency and com-

---

[4] https://www.techtarget.com/sustainability/feature/Top-ESG-reporting-frameworks-explained-and-compared

pleteness of ESG-related information disclosed in their reports. The European Parliament has issued two main directives on ESG reporting rules, the Non-Financial Reporting Directive (NFRD) of 2014 and the more recent Corporate Sustainability Reporting Directive (CSRD), approved in November 2022, which took effect in January 2023. The NFRD applied only to public interest entities with more than 500 employees in the EU, reaching a pool of around 6,000 companies and groups.[5] It required companies to integrate their annual reports with non-financial statements including information on their commitment to environmental protection, social responsibility, human rights protection, treatment of workers, board diversity, bribery and anti-corruption policies.

5.4   Greenwashing, Greenhushing and Greenbleaching

As we've seen, the term "greenwashing" is commonly used to refer to a company's practice of misleading consumers about the positive environmental impact of its operations or products. The aim is to deceive consumers into believing that a company or its products are "environmentally friendly" when in fact they are not, and to profit from doing so. The term was first used in 1986 by Jay Westerveld, an American biologist and environmentalist, to refer to the hotel industry's practice of reusing bath towels, ostensibly for environmental reasons, when the real purpose was to save on laundry costs.

Today, the term "greenwashing" has a broader meaning, encompassing a variety of behaviors and spanning all sectors of the business world. The phenomenon has also spread dramatically. In fact, the EU Commission estimates[6] that:

- 53% of green claims are misleading and unclear
- 40% of green claims are unsupported by evidence
- 50% of green labels have little or no verification

---

[5] https://www.greenfinanceplatform.org/policies-and-regulations/non-financial-reporting-directive-nfrd-directive-201495eu-and-proposal#:~:text=The%20European%20Union%20(EU)%20Directive,of%20employees%2C%20respect%20for%20human

[6] https://environment.ec.europa.eu/topics/circular-economy/green-claims_en

- There are approximately 230 sustainability labels and 100 green energy labels in the EU, with widely varying levels of transparency

"Companies need data transparency with detailed precision along the entire value chain. They have to act quickly as ESG frameworks and standards evolve, embedding into every business process sustainability metrics that are aligned with the company strategy" said Deborah Kaplan,[7] the global head of sustainability at SAP Customer Success.

An anonymous survey conducted by Harris Poll[8] for Google Cloud asked nearly 1,500 CEOs and C-suite executives at companies with more than 500 employees about their role in addressing climate change. When asked about their commitment to sustainability, 58 percent of executives globally and 68 percent in the U.S. said their companies are guilty of greenwashing. And two-thirds of global executives questioned whether their company's sustainability efforts were genuine.

There have been some major scandals involving greenwashing practices in the past. One of the most famous involves the German carmaker Volkswagen. In 2009, VW launched a marketing campaign to promote its "clean diesel" cars, claiming that some brand-new Audi models had drastically reduced emissions, as evidenced by special software installed in the cars that tracked emissions.

The U.S. Environmental Protection Agency (EPA) discovered in 2014 that these software devices had actually been manipulated to appear to comply with EPA emissions directives during test runs, while in reality they would switch to a different mode of operation during normal use, reporting a false (lower) level of emissions. In fact, emissions were found to be 40 times higher than the federal limit. The so called "Diesel-gate" scandal cost Volkswagen about $40 billion.[9]

Many companies made bold claims about being environmentally conscious for marketing purposes, but made no serious sustainability efforts. Many others were doing the right thing, but in the shadows, there is another troubling corporate sustainability trend called "greenhushing".

---

[7] Alice Ross, «Sustainability Trends 2023: Goodbye Greenwashing, Hello Business Results», *Forbes*, January 31st 2023.

[8] Founded in 1956, The Harris Poll is one of the longest running surveys in the U.S. tracking public opinion, motivations, and social sentiments.

[9] https://www.nrdc.org/stories/what-greenwashing

This is when a company doesn't publicize its environmental achievements because it does not want to be called out when it falls short of its stated goals. Unlike greenwashing, in which companies exaggerate their sustainable policies, greenhushers keep their sustainability policies quiet. A 2022 report by the climate consultancy South Pole found that of the 1,200 private companies it surveyed that are considered global climate leaders, nearly a quarter do not disclose their environmental achievements and milestones.

In the UK, the Financial Conduct Authority (FCA) plans to announce new rules in mid-2023 on which funds are considered sustainable, as part of its Sustainable Disclosure Requirements (SDR). According to the *Financial Times*,[10] while the fund management industry insists on the need to crack down on greenwashing, it fears that the rules will be so restrictive that some funds it considers sustainable will not be able to be labeled as such. So it is fighting back with a term of its own: "greenbleaching."

Greenbleaching refers to financial market participants who choose not to disclose the ESG characteristics of their products in order to avoid additional regulation and potential legal risks. The term already gained popularity in early 2023, when the Securities and Markets Stakeholder Group (SMSG), in response to a call for evidence on greenwashing by the European Securities and Markets Authority (ESMA), stressed the importance for EU authorities to ensure that any new rules on greenwashing that are ratified also protect against greenbleaching.

Organizations are characterized by zeal. When they adopt a new methodology, they execute it diligently, with intensity and, to some extent, with extremism. Over time, such practices become a panacea, an unshakable problem-solving creed that, if questioned or challenged, can prompt accusations of blasphemy. This has happened in the past, for example, with BPR (Business Process Reengineering), the Balanced Score Card, or GE's Six Sigma. ESG is no exception, with the added push of modern media and social networking; the rate of awareness and adoption is unprecedented.

By 2022, more than $35 trillion in assets globally were monitored using sustainability criteria, an increase of 55% since 2016. CEOs of S&P

---

[10] Alice Ross, «Sustainable investors don't need 'green bleaching'», *Financial Times*, March 22, 2023.

500 companies mention ESG very frequently, to be perceived as honorary members of the ESG club: an average of nine times per quarter on earnings calls, up from once, if at all, in 2017.[11]

Global ESG assets may surpass $50 trillion by 2025, one-third of the projected total assets under management globally, according to a new report by Bloomberg Intelligence (BI).[12]

ESG is not without its critics and its aura of purity is currently being challenged. In the U.S., the concept has become politicized and divisive. On March 1st, 2023, the Senate voted to overturn a Labor Department rule allowing pension funds to consider ESG criteria when making investment decisions, following a similar vote by House Republicans on February 28.[13] Critics of ESG argue that investments are based on political agendas rather than on generating the best returns for savers. Conservative lawmakers tend to view the strategy with suspicion. "ESG is really antithetical to our American way of life, to our Constitution," said Republican state Rep. Barbara Ehardt. In early 2022, lawmakers in Idaho, a Republican-held state, passed a law preventing ESG considerations from overriding state requirements that investments be made according to the prudent investor rule. [14]

The use of ESG has gone from a magnet for trillions of dollars of investments to make the corporate world more transparent and save the climate to a source of bitterness and distrust. Claims such as "ESG is at the heart of everything we do" have become a common selling line, as if a simple statement could make a wish come true. It's like the joke told by a former Egyptian telecommunication minister during a conference in early 2000 on the indispensability of the Internet. With the same zealous logic, every actor added an "e" to all activities to underline the adherence to the then new digital mantra. The minister said on stage: "In my country we have solved the problem from the atop, from today we will be E-gypt."

In 2022, a special report on ESG by *The Economist* argued that ESG is a broken system in desperate need of repair if its noble early days ambi-

---

[11] "Bank of International Settlements", *The Economist*, Sep 29th, 2022.

[12] «ESG May Surpass $41 Trillion Assets in 2022, But Not Without Challenges, Finds Bloomberg Intelligence», Bloomberg.com, January 24, 2022.

[13] *Fortune*, March 1, 2023.

[14] The Associated Press (AP), Nov 21, 2022.

tions are to be saved: "The environmental, social and governance (ESG) approach to investment is broken. It needs to be streamlined and stripped of sanctimoniousness."[15] Some Wall Street giants are also becoming less passionate about ESG. JPMorgan Chase and Morgan Stanley seriously considered leaving the Glasgow Financial Alliance for Net Zero (GFANZ). Some actions have been taken, such as changing the standards of some members. However, two pension funds, Australia's Cbus Super and Austria's Bundespensionkasse, have already left[16].

As mentioned earlier, ESG was developed for companies to apply its principles, which focus on the three pillars of environmental, social, and governance. Through ESG, the private sector sought to fill the gap left by policymakers and respond to stakeholders' environmental concerns. A similar attempt was made with the GBDe episode described earlier in this book. Once again, the primacy of politics has proven not to be fungible with any other constituency.

It is up to policymakers to apply the right dose of regulatory pressure to make ESG better: more accurate, standardized information, working with the private sector to define a set of common measures of size that make ratings less subjective. This would allow the industry to be accountable and not to overpromise and underdeliver.

Assuming the above is achievable, however, ESG does not address the broader societal problem and the specific need for policymakers to be informed, and thus for a more equitable media.

In conclusion, the JP Morgan CEO's call to action – "governments need help" – remains true and relevant. The IRG offers a realistic solution in which the ten parameters analyzed belong strictly to business. The IRG fully recognizes that policymakers are in need of understanding and does not attempt to be a substitute for politics. Rather, the IRG's primary goal is to inform elected officials.

---

[15] Henry Tricks, *The Economist* - Schumpeter column.
[16] *The Economist*, Sep 29, 2022.

6   The IRG Metric: A Step into a New Future

6.1   An Introduction

Through its strategic plan, a company speaks to and engages with the society or societies in which it operates. Addressing the structural changes in national and international society described so far requires a number of steps.

The purpose of the IRG is to keep the company aligned and on track to deliver sustainable results, while helping other players (such as policymakers and governments) address and inoculate against societal imbalances.

Artificial Intelligence (AI) is a current challenge for the world and especially for policymakers. AI will affect all industries. The nightmare scenario is that its full implementation will cause massive harm.

There are advocates and skeptics. Supporters tend to emphasize the positive aspects of AI, such as its role in developing new medicines, helping to combat climate change, or generating clean and safe nuclear energy. Skeptics, on the other hand, fear a world of super-intelligent machines overtaking humans.

One U.S. senator dryly but effectively described the level of preparedness of regulators to deal with AI: "To be honest, Congress doesn't know what the hell it's doing in this area."[1] In his view, lawmakers do not understand the technology, so they should listen to the experts. AI raises real concerns about media bias, privacy, and intellectual property rights,

---

[1] Ted Cruz US Senator, June 15, 2023, interview by *Politico*, Editor-in-Chief Matt Kaminski.

among others. Microsoft and Google, for example, with their $5 trillion market capitalization, are commercially active with their AI-powered products that will help users create documents and perform other tasks.

AI is a good example of where the IRG applies. It could help companies that are currently forging AI (along with universities, research centers, and domain experts) to play a central role in sharing knowledge with policymakers and raising awareness among stakeholders on the challenges and opportunities. AI will impact the jobs of the future, it will require retraining of the workforce, it will be applied to armaments and, of course, it will increase cybersecurity threats. Whatever regulatory approach is chosen – from a light touch to full regulation – it must be based on a comprehensive and competent understanding to balance the opportunities of AI with an assessment of the risks and a mitigation strategy.

The IRG is a strategic system anchored on business realism, both in methodology and process. It helps the organization develop, refine, and drive the goals and themes of its strategic plan in a way that is fully understood and appreciated by stakeholders.

Times are changing, and the contribution of this methodology is timely in a world best described by the American economist Jeffrey D. Sachs:

> *"All countries — including the United States, members of the European Union, Russia, China, Iran, and, yes, Afghanistan — are destabilized by the COVID-19 pandemic; the effects of the climate crisis (floods, droughts, hurricanes, forest fires, heatwaves); widening income inequality further dividing the haves and have nots; the upheavals of digital technologies; and the dangerous political influence of plutocrats. All of these are shared problems across the globe, and all require intensive global cooperation rather than confrontation.".[2]*

Through this methodology, the company becomes focused and effective in its broader social environment. It plays both a proactive and defensive role, avoiding controversy through managed engagement. It enables the company to delimit its sphere of possible intervention to those issues that are related and tangential to its core business. This avoids stakeholder expectations of messianic performance, while allowing for carefully managed additional engagement in the broader arena, where the corporation's high skills can be effective without controversy. This process also

---

[2] Jeffrey D. Sachs, *Boston Globe*, September 3, 2021.

precludes the opposite controversy: the perception of the uncaring and socially blind corporation with a narrow focus solely on profit.

In general, traditional business does not act out of a higher sense of justice, holiness, or social mission. It responds to needs, with the best organizations trying to anticipate them. Most companies are not designed to manage the emerging social demands and concerns that were previously tangential to their core business: but the challenges are getting tougher, society is expressing anxieties, and these concerns now have a deep sense of urgency. Responding effectively and holistically to these unmet needs is also cost-effective. It is no longer just a matter of profit and loss, as the fundamental long-term viability of a business is inextricably linked to the stability of the environment in which it operates. This stability is itself a driver of value, and must therefore be preserved.

As we will see, this is not just the job of top management. It requires a new organizational culture to engage employees; training to create a set of new skills; new processes so that all parties involved in and around the company – can understand, appreciate and manage the change that must take place in order to be aligned with and responsive to the societal changes that have already occurred, as previously illustrated. The current way in which a company presents itself to the outside world needs to be re-examined according to the IRG parameters and its internal behavior. The scope of this cultural shift must encompass the universities that educate future generations, the media to provide an additional perspective to decipher the current societal changes, the various NGOs involved, and of course the policymakers. This evolution takes time, and the IRG parameters provide both the measurements and the underlying values to bring about this change.

To further verify the strength and logic of the IRG approach, its strategy, its metrics, and its level of its pragmatism, I met with more than twenty CEOs and thought leaders in Europe and the United States. These conversations reinforced the understanding of the IRG as a strong, pragmatic, and welcome solution to the unique business dilemmas of today. These CEOs and thought leaders were able to envision the structural social, environmental and economic changes taking place now and in the future, and how the public expectations of CEOs have risen as a result of the increased trust and expectations now placed on them.

6.2   How is the IRG Metric Structured?
The Rationale behind the Parameters

Richard Haass, President Emeritus of the Council on Foreign Relations, observed:

> *"A business leader today must do more than worry about profits… what they need to do is talk about how to increase the odds that conditions exist in which their businesses can operate successfully."*[3]

A number of questions arise from this statement:

- Are companies aligned with this rapidly changing social construct?
- Are companies confident that stakeholders understand what they stand for and the strategic direction and associated cost-benefit trade-offs?
- Are companies prepared to improve their dialogue with the media and provide the general public with more accessible information and knowledge about the issues at hand?
- Are companies equipped to lead in new arenas, to respond to the growing pressure of public opinion, and to re-orient themselves as value-adding partners in society?
- Are companies able to work with non-corporate actors such as policymakers and, where appropriate, transfer the necessary know-how to them, while avoiding confrontation and controversy?
- Have companies developed a plan for the coming new environment that is quantifiable, measurable, achievable, and also safe and prosperous for the company?
- How does a company ensure that employees of all backgrounds feel safe enough to maximize their creativity, innovation, and productivity?
- How does the CEO ensure that the board has proper oversight of these critical issues? How does the corporate culture adapt to this new world?

The IRG prepares top and middle management to answer these ques-

---

[3] Richard Haass, President Emeritus of the Council on Foreign Relations, interviewed by *The Voice of Business* in New York on May 2019.

tions, with the ambition to plan for a better future, to act on a focused path forward, and to be aware of the pitfalls as well as the benefits.

To avoid presenting readers with an unnecessarily detailed operational manual of the IRG, here is an overview of the IRG methodology, starting with the 10 measurable parameters, each generating a rating of 1 to 3 being 30 the perfect score:

Figure 6.1   The 10 parameters of the IRG.[4]

1	Company governance
	Measures the soundness of the company's governance, the capabilities/suitability of its board members to support its mission, its structure, and related evaluation processes

2	Industry leadership
	Measures the impact of the company within its own sector(s)

3	Financial influence
	Measures the financial strength of the enterprise

4	Industry power
	Measures the company's position in shaping the terms of the debate domestically/ regionally and/or globally beyond its own sector(s) and/or adjacent sectors

5	Innovation excellence
	Focuses on the company's role as a global innovator within the industry

6	World citizenship
	Measures the company's actions, presence and leadership in key national and international fora; addressing global/regional/ local sustainable and innovative issues for societal/industry well-being; becoming a thought-leader and sought-after partner/advisor

7	Media strength
	Measures the company's ability to communicate the 2-3 strategic issues that contribute to societal well-being; to engage and enhance the understanding of its stakeholders, including policymakers; to promote its global citizenship vision in a "statesman-like" manner; to be perceived as a competent advisor on how to honor/ address the issues at stake

(follows)

---

[4] Trademark/Service Mark Statement of Use (15 U.S.C. Section 1051(d)) To the Commissioner for Trademarks: MARK: IRG INDEX; SERIAL NUMBER: 87569154. For International Class 035: Current identification: Compiling indexes of information used for gauging and assessing the influence of a country, city, region, or company.

(continues)

8	Thought leadership
	The company's ability to contribute to industry/management development with cutting edge best practices and opinions, and to communicate these to external constituencies. It creates the means/media to share its vision and know-how with stakeholders and especially with policymakers

9	Social responsibility/diversity/sustainability
	The organization's plans and approach to supporting these issues internally (workplace) and externally

10	Human capital
	Measures the attractiveness of the organization as a workplace/employer and its efforts to support employees' professional development, attract talent, and responding to emerging needs.

These ten parameters profile a company that is ready to respond to and help other constituencies meet the challenges that are part of or tangential to its core business. The IRG describes a more extroverted company, aware of its strengths and the need to share its knowledge with a more informed audience of stakeholders. Such an organization is also aware of the power of the media and emphasizes the freedom and autonomy of each constituent. It combines the ability to learn with the fulfillment of other needs and the perceived utility of the knowledge by stakeholders. AI represents a point at which policymakers seek support. Because AI is a cross-industry and cross-social phenomenon, companies must proactively address this understanding gap to avoid an anxious public pushing policymakers to react rather than lead.

For a company to be IRG fit must score 20 or higher.

The Leadership

The first five parameters measure the strength and leadership of a company. Starting with its governance characteristics and comparing them to best practices, they determine a company's standing and influence within its own industry.

An influential company performs financially to reward its shareholders and be valued by the financial community. However, the company's power should be perceived and appreciated beyond its industry. An influential and relevant company is one of the leaders in the debate, helping to the identify both domestic and international strategic issues that impact local and global society. For example, cybersecurity is a challenge that only innovation can address. Asymmetrical cyber warfare can be extremely disruptive and costly for all parties involved, making continuous dialogue and cooperation between companies and government agencies essential.

Responsiveness to market inputs

According to parameters six and seven – "World Citizenship" and "Media Strength" – an influential and relevant company is an active participant in those global and regional forums that conceive and shape opinion and impact on relevant issues: climate change, energy transition, pharmaceuticals, education, health, poverty alleviation, inequality, food security, cybersecurity, artificial intelligence, national security, job security, economic recovery, job opportunities for the next generation, financial and banking regulation, and all those concerns that contribute to global stability and prosperity.

Based on its core business expertise and vision, the company helps people understand what is at stake and what must be done collectively to address existing and emerging challenges. This prominence allows an influential and relevant company to be a sought-after problem solver and inspiration for policymakers, and the IRG addresses how to manage this interface.

An important aspect is "media strength," which measures how well the company communicates the relevant strategies and critical issues it is working on for the benefit of all. This parameter does not take into account day-to-day commercial and financial communications.

Empowerment to act

Parameter eight measures a corporation's thought leadership in practice, including how it disseminates knowledge and how it works creatively and openly with policymakers to inform them of the challenges ahead. Parameters nine and ten deal with human capital, which is a company's ethos in managing resources and people across the value chain. This includes empowerment – the ability and effectiveness to make every employee an agent of change. Workplace quality, racial equity, child care, and mental health are now top of mind for CEOs. To quote one of the most influential business leaders of our time, BlackRock's Larry Fink,

CEOs *"must be thoughtful about how they use their voice and connect on social issues important to their employees."*[5]

An influential and relevant company makes innovation and knowledge creation a central part of its strategy. Thought leadership must be learned and used wisely to properly disseminate innovation widely, thereby creating the appropriate level of understanding and appreciation (in concert with the previous parameters).

Social responsibility, diversity, and sustainability are integral parts of being an influential and relevant player and are evaluated accordingly. Parameters six, seven, and eight, taken together, provide an assessment of a company's ability and effectiveness to build bridges with other stakeholders and to effectively transfer its knowledge to policymakers.

By analyzing the business and proactively using the IRG indicators, top management will be able to measure and direct corporate alignment through a system that continually adapt to the rapidly changing expectations, needs, and structure of society.

The IRG indicators will provide managers with an up-to-date view of the company, its health and its ability to meet societal needs. Protecting the economic and environmental stability of that society should be seen as a corporate act of intelligent self-interest and long-term profitability.

By working with the IRG, the company will gain the sensors, skills, human resources profile, and the risk-averse positioning to lead and respond to emerging needs before they escalate, and to develop the ability to contribute to and shape the solutions. In practice, the IRG becomes an integral part of the strategic plan, enriching and strengthening it by considering issues and sensitivities overlooked by older approaches. In this way, the corporate strategic plan serves the company and is tailored to the social geography in which it must ultimately land.

6.3   The Distinguishing Methodology of IRG

The IRG methodology is articulated into three phases: (1) company self-assessment, (2) market analysis, and (3) action plan. The three phases are as follows:

---

[5] Larry Fink's, *Letter to CEOs: The Power of Capitalism*, 2022.

1. Pragmatic Analysis and Deliverables. In the first phase, designated top management has the opportunity to assess the corporation in relation to ten metrics, each of which generates a rating of 1 to 3. This analysis is collaborative and confidential.

2. Objective Market Assessment. In the second phase, the same ten metrics are assessed against the market using AI software, again with a rating of 1 to 3. This uses comprehensive industry data and benchmarking criteria, both within the industry and externally, to identify best practices. A detailed understanding of the company's influence, the relevance of the company's current areas of focus, and its contribution to ensuring economic growth is then generated. This proprietary software is based on machine learning and artificial intelligence and provides thorough and statistically significant market analysis.

3. Action Plan: in this third and final phase, a company can visualize the difference that exists between the self-assessment, which is typically more optimistic, and what the stakeholders believe. AI software makes the external analysis very robust and allows top management to identify areas for improvement and design the appropriate action plan. As mentioned earlier, a company must score 20 or above in order to be IRG fit.

Sentiment Analysis and Key Performance Indicators help us score the company on the 10 dimensions of the IRG, as summarized in the Table 6.1.

The following is a high-level explanation of the steps required to implement the IRG:

- AI software (Fig. 6.1).
- A sanitized example of the breadth and depth of the market analysis enabled by distributed computing (Fig. 6.2).
- The filtering process that allows distillation and selection of data relevant to the IRG (Fig. 6.3).
- The normalization process (Fig. 6.4).

The market analysis is performed by proprietary AI software. The graph illustrates the sequence of actions required to obtain the final IRG score. It should be noted that to have correct and unbiased machine learning, human supervision is required to ensure that the algorithms are correct

Table 6.1   Sentiment analysis and key performance indicators

Topic modelling and Sentiment analysis General and specialized traditional media and social media	Key performance indicators (KPIs) Corporate reports, press releases, public rankings, and databases
We use topic modeling to understand what themes the public refers to when talking about the company and its peers. We use sentiment analysis to understand how the public feels about these topics. This allows us to determine the public's overall opinion of the company and its peers in the panel. Specifically, we have: • Scraped the web for all different sources related to the companies • Filtered out irrelevant content • Discovered and assigned subtopics to each of the IRG dimensions • Calculated the net sentiment at the IRG dimension level	KPIs taken from corporate communications and public databases allow the company to be mapped to the dimensions of the IRG. These KPIs are used to complement the results of topic modeling and sentiment analysis. Examples of such KPIs are: • Presence in ESG rankings • Number of awards • Number of patents • Economic and financial performance

Source: Kearney and NeWest

and performing the task for which they were written. Topic identification, opinion scoring and data mining are AI-driven once human oversight has ensured the required quality and data integrity.

Below is an anonymized client example that demonstrates the breadth and depth of the analysis, using AI to leverage different types of sources to understand how the companies are viewed from an influence and relevance perspective.

The company and selected peers are unbalanced in size and operate in different businesses. Normalization is therefore required to compare players on content (total, filtered, and IRG-related fragments) and KPIs.

The normalization is based on the most appropriate driver for each dimension of the IRG. Where applicable, the same driver is used for simplicity and comprehension.

Figure 6.1 AI software

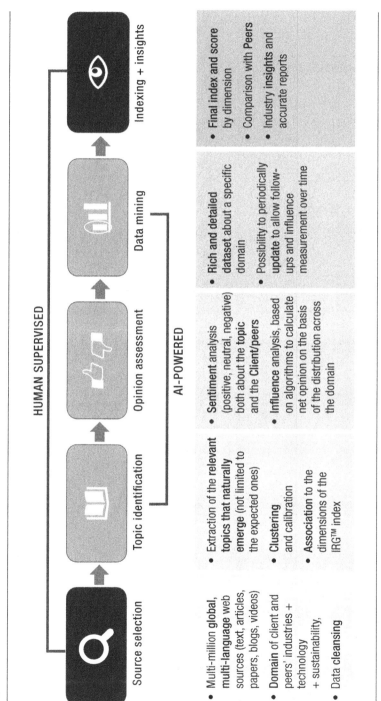

HUMAN SUPERVISED

| Source selection | Topic identification | Opinion assessment | Data mining | Indexing + insights |

AI-POWERED

- Multi-million **global, multi-language** web sources (text, articles, papers, blogs, videos)
- **Domain** of client and peers' industries + technology + sustainability,
- **Data cleansing**

- **Extraction of the relevant topics that naturally emerge** (not limited to the expected ones)
- **Clustering** and calibration
- **Association** to the dimensions of the IRG™ index

- **Sentiment** analysis (positive, neutral, negative) both about the **topic** and the **Client/peers**
- **Influence** analysis, based on algorithms to calculate net opinion on the basis of the distribution across the domain

- **Rich and detailed dataset** about a specific domain
- **Possibility** to periodically **update** to allow follow-ups and influence measurement over time

- **Final index and score** by dimension
- **Comparison with Peers**
- Industry **insights** and accurate reports

Source: Kearney, NEWEST

Figure 6.2

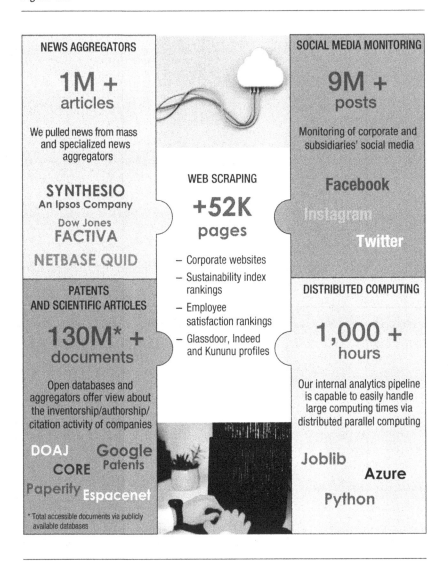

Figure 6.3

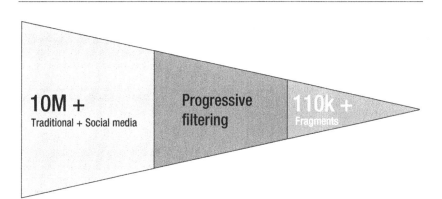

Total content	Filtered content	Total fragments relevant for the IRG
Total Traditional and Social media that have been scraped from the Web in relation to FS Group and peer companies in the panel. The research has been done on different sources, as previously illustrated.	Filter out non relevant content for the panel companies. The progressive filtering removed: • Mis-leading content, such as homonyms and synonyms on players and topics; • Duplicated contents, that are replicated by multiple sources; • Content whose attribution to the player is doubtful; • Contents not related to the scope of the IRG.	Select content relevant for IRG category: the fragments are the portions of content (up to three subsequent sentences) where both the company and one of the IRG topics are mentioned.

Source: Kearney, NEWEST

Figure 6.4   IRG Normalization applied

Normalization on cash cost	Normalization on employees	Normalization on followers
Cost normalization is used for all IRG dimensions, except Human Capital and Media Power.	The Human Capital dimension refers to employee-related topics.	The Media Power dimension includes both traditional and social media related topics.
The cash costs are computed for each player as:		
Cash Cost = Opex + Investments		
To normalize a value, it is divided by the costs of the relative player:	The most appropriate way to normalize this dimension is to use the number of employees of each player:	The most appropriate way to normalize the social media content and fragments is to use the number of followers of each player:
$Value_{norm} = \dfrac{Value}{Cost}$	$Value_{norm} = \dfrac{Value}{\#\ of\ employees}$	$Value_{norm} = \dfrac{Value}{\#\ of\ followers}$

Source: Kearney, NEWEST

The Table 6.1 illustrates the IRG methodology applied to a sanitized client example.

Following the market research results, the parameters converge into four transformation programs to enhance the company's Influence, Relevance and Growth from its original baseline. Each transformation program is designed to improve the performance of one or more IRG parameters:

The implementation of these four transformation programs will increase the IRG score from 16 to 21/23.

Table 6.1 IRG methodology applied

Transformation program	Brief Description	IRG Parameters Involved
Statesman Role & Positioning	Develop key influential topics and communicate properly to position the company as enabler of the energy transition	Industry Leadership, Industry Power, World Citizenship, Media Power
	Focus on key stakeholder through a new operating model	
	Support Internationalization of selected suppliers	
	Strengthen relationship/presence on key media and social	
Digital Transformation	Redesign digitalization initiatives into a holistic Digital Transformation program	Innovation Excellence, Human Capital
	Review and integrate digital initiatives in core Business across the value chain	
	Enhance digitalization in core staff functions: employee journeys, planning, control, and reporting	
Innovation & Though Leadership	Pursue initiatives in the Innovation Plan and finalize design of new Innovation units	Industry Leadership, Thought Leadership, Media Power, Innovation Excellence
	Exploit the opportunity of patenting, to gain external recognition and create advantage in "new" markets	
	Establish a Knowledge Management System to disseminate knowledge and foster innovation	
Human Capital & Diversity	Complete design and implementation of world-class recruiting	Social Responsibility/ Diversity, Sustainability, Human Capital
	Increase Diversity of workforce (gender, nationalities, university background)	
	Redefine Performance Management & Development	
	Achieve external recognition as top-employer	

Source: Kearney, NEWEST

Figure 6.5   IRG scoring example

		Current score	Target score
🏛	1. Company governance	3	3
	2. Industry leadership	2	3
	3. Financial influence	3	3
	4. Industry power	1	1-2
	5. Innovation excellence	1	2
	6. World Citizenship	1	2
	7. Media Strength	1	2
	8. Thought Leadership	1	1-2
	9. Social Resp/Div./Sust.	2	2
	10. Human capital	1	2
	Total score	**16**	**21-23**

Source: Kearney, Newest

To achieve the transformation recommended by the IRG analyses, the company created an organizational unit reporting to the CEO, specifically tasked with:

- Establishing a Program Management Office (PMO) reporting to the CEO.
- Appointing a PMO leader, supported by two dedicated resources.
- Appointing the key initiative leaders for each stream and/or inter-functional covering the organizational units involved.
- Launching individual initiatives according to plan.

The transformation programs identified a number of detailed action plans for each program. Figure 6.6 is an illustrative selection of such actions per transformation program to be managed by the PMO.

Figure 6.6 IRG Action plan

# of Initiative	Action Plan
Statesman Role 1.1 (preparatory)	Develop 3 versions per key theme to position as an enabler of: 1. Market …, 2. Security …, 3. Technology development …: Select the 3 versions per topic through internal meetings: engineering, strategy, communications, ICT as key input leaders; ensure a "simple language" Plan for the development of a pipeline of content/position papers for each key topic Assign each content/position paper to a lead developer Select authoritative third parties as needed (….) for the external validation of position papers, when needed for objectivity of research Monitor delivery of content / position papers according to plan
1.2	Strengthen presence in key domestic and international media outlets and leverage social media to increase media and industry power: Identify a list of domestic and international media outlets that would be interested in/beneficial to an IRG partnership with the company Define IRG Partnership MoU principles and objectives, media benefits, the company principles– no play for play, etc. In collaboration with selected media design innovative content programs (brainstorming out of the box, identifying best practices that have created/changed user habits/contributed to culture) to support policymakers and have a more informed stakeholder base Select a leading international PR/marketing agency for actions in … references, identify slate of topics, launch tender, select induction (critical to refine the scope appropriately as they are not used to) Define Influence Communication Strategy & Plan (traditional and social media) to increase top management qualified exits (articles, interviews, posts) to ~200 in key … media (from <100), to ~50 in key international media, to ~500 in key social media (from ~150) Review internal capabilities and managers fit for the task, if necessary, consider hiring a manager Identify spokesperson(s) for each content/paper to maximize reach Allocate time for key spokesperson(s) to: meet one-on-one with selected senior journalists in … organize press conference in … to launch "Statesman" campaign with high quality national and international media; select key issues to communicate during Capital Market Day(s) Adjust content by media and communicate

(follows)

(continues)

# of Initiative	Action Plan
1.3 a	Focus on key stakeholders – Strengthen role in industry sector association to achieve industry leadership: Select key issues and identify key committees/working groups Map relevant activities and identify key meetings/dates Select and deploy key resources, give them clear objectives Define reporting and regular updates with top management. Execute, monitor and adjust
1.3 b	Focus on key stakeholders – Review role in current associations, think tanks and gatherings to achieve industry leadership, industry power and global citizenship: Finalize selection of associations and think tanks through top management meeting Select key referents and define objectives through selected key associations Design modalities for participation by selected key gatherings Identify spokesperson for each meeting – aim to increase qualified top management participation (speeches, round-tables) to 50 key international meetings (from ~25) Regular preparation/participation in … gatherings: Restate … goal & strategy: review and integrate action plan proposed by S. Helm Meeting with … (week of Nov. 5) on … agenda by … and conf call with … underway; select key company spokesperson(s) for XXX events Prepare for and attend summit in New York (week of …) Identify best option(s) for impactful … event for CEO Prepare and attend … Forum week (year xxx) Prepare think-tank event for CEO in the same week
1.3 c	Focus on key stakeholders – fine-tune role in NGOs and CSR association to enhance global citizenship status: Assess participation in CSR … and finalize selection through a top management meeting Select key referents and define objectives through selected key association Refine modalities of participation by selected key meeting Identify a spokesperson for each key meeting Execute, monitor and adjust Align strategy/action/timing with previous steps to ensure efficient implementation

(follows)

(continues)

# of Initiative	Action Plan
1.4	Support the internationalization of selected supply chain players to achieve industry leadership and power:
	Suppliers selection: shortlist via internal meetings with business and functional leaders
	Approach, visit and negotiate with 2-3 selected suppliers
	Design a master plan on how to educate the suppliers: SWOT analysis for each and tailored solution for each
	Launch specific initiatives
	Induction session(s) leading to a well-planned company Internationalization Day, also to be used for communication purposes (Statesman role)
	Introduction to key local stakeholders and support in building local network
	Support for local establishment, hiring, training, etc.
	Regular analysis of impact (e.g. increase in turnover, increase in employment)
	Alert and support communication in leveraging impact with institutional stakeholders and key traditional/social media
	On-going/planned initiatives in Innovation Plan
	Develop and implement Innovation plan according to current processes
2.1	Partner with key universities to increase innovation excellence, thought leadership and human capital:
	Select top universities in Europe (3-4, likely 2 in DACH, 1 in Benelux and UK) and globally (likely another 1-2 in the US)
	Prepare a strategy pitch: why joining the company's strategy is a value-add for them
	Identify who to talk to: Approach them with proposal for both research and recruitment
	Negotiate terms of agreement
	Launch specific initiatives as agreed
2.2	Develop patents to increase innovation excellence, media power and industry leadership (especially abroad).
	Review innovation process to assess patentability as additional criteria for selecting initiatives.
	Design patent office and issue organizational directive.
	Select legal / operational support.
	Search for patent opportunities among past R&D projects and recent innovations already in operation.
	Organize and conduct an event with relevant employees where patentability criteria are explained by legal counsel and the relevance of patenting is explained by top management to create awareness, motivation and change.
	Review the patentability of recent internal R&D initiatives.

6.4   The IRG and Innovative Media

The IRG provides companies with the metrics to measure and adapt to the extraordinary changes taking place in society. A similar approach is needed when dealing with the media, both traditional and digital, requiring new platforms to serve, amplify and reach the appropriate audience.

The Media Strength metric measures a company's ability to master the communication of its strategic intent and purpose.[6] It focuses on assessing whether there is sufficient and understandable communication to explain the company's efforts to ensure that its strategic plans are known and appreciated by its stakeholders.

Television remains the key medium for reaching a broad audience, whether viewed on a traditional TV screen, a computer screen, or a hand-held device. Traditional advertising campaigns are still the preferred choice of established companies to build awareness. Scaling from TV to digital remains the preferred path, not the other way around.

In addition, established think tanks are looking for ways to use new technology platforms to engage and reach a broader audience in order to remain policy-rich change agents. While face-to-face meetings are back and human interaction remains a critical feature of relationship building, the media continues to provide the window through which complex issues are communicated and made attractive to a wider audience. Media channels enable and invites an active participation in the most relevant debates, providing more knowledge and, over time, more competence.

As we have seen earlier, stakeholders and employees expect CEOs to be more visible and vocal on issues not only related to a firm's core business, but also those that are tangential to it. In their perceived areas of expertise, CEOs are now expected to inform policymakers on key economic and societal issues. Satisfying these new societal demands requires the support of the media and selected think tanks. This step is critical to creating awareness, demonstrating competence, and disseminating knowledge that can inform policymakers.

---

[6] Unless requested, traditional advertising and financial communication is excluded from analysis as standard internal corporate departmental practices.

Accordingly, the IRG is reaching out to the media. It has launched a website, Newest, where the editorial line and the interviews with business leaders and thought leaders reflect its approach to influence, relevance and growth.[7]

In addition, in partnership with CNBC as media partner and the world-renowned leadership organizations The Aspen Institute in the US and Aspen Institute Italia, it will launch an innovative annual symposium that will bring together the world's most influential CEOs and thought leaders to discuss solutions to the most pressing issues. This will allow leaders Newest to reach a wider audience and provide a follow-up via CNBC to verify concrete action. The symposiums will address the issues that matter most to stakeholders. This format, combined with the "slice and dice" nature of the digital world, creates a greater opportunity to shape and respond to the broader expectations of companies in society.

Making complex news more accessible to a broader audience is part of the IRG's programmatic way forward to assess, create and lead a manageable future.

6.5   The IRG and the Future

The IRG is an innovative yet timely methodology that allows corporations to adapt to a new social structure characterized by a high trust in such corporations and NGOs and low trust in media and government.

These constituencies are the cornerstones of democracy, and each has a particular trait or mission that it must fulfill in order to be a credible and respected constituent.

Globalization has is some ways undermined the equitable distribution of talented resources and, because it is based on the rule of international law, has required less government or public sector involvement. The value proposition offered by the private sector over the past 30 years – compensation, career advancement, depth and speed of work experience, internationalization – has attracted most of the available talent pool. Corporations have made good use of these resources and have become large, global and financially sound. The public sector has

---

[7] www.newestcorp.com

suffered and failed to "fight back," so that today the quality of parliamentarians and staff across the spectrum is not up to the ethical complexities of the world.

Governments seem neither competent nor capable of dealing with the issues at hand, failing some of the essential traits of this constituent. This is a reality shared by all democracies, with significant peaks in the U.S. and Europe.

Many CEOs from the United States, and increasingly from Europe, have become publicly vocal on this issue. This is not because of any particular virtue; rather, stakeholders are demanding that CEOs engage and act on issues such as labor, climate, and discrimination. CEOs need a stable and predictable environment to compete and create wealth. Policymakers, in turn, should provide such stability and predictability.

The IRG is one possible answer as leaders recognize that the alternative solutions, including ESG, were not designed to address this specific challenge. Indeed, stakeholders realize that business and government must work together to achieve better and more concrete solutions.[8] This approach is possible for companies that belong to a democracy, whether complete or flawed one, as the Democracy Index shows. Only democracies nurture these four constituencies, albeit with varying degrees of efficiency and success.

Furthermore, the IRG approach allows a corporation to openly share its limitations in order to address expectations that sometimes become messianic. In today's world, it is important to define, in a timely manner and before a crisis erupts, what is feasible and compatible with the realm of business and what is not. The demand and pressures on corporations, especially in the U.S., are growing and so intense that one can be easily be drawn in unwelcome partisan and political territory. Businesses can certainly assist (inform) policymakers in fulfilling their social justice obligations and help address the ethical dilemmas posed by new technological frontiers and inclusion.

As illustrated, the IRG takes ESG into account and ensures that this practice continues to be applied and respected, ensuring the long-term sustainability of any collaboration.

---

[8] 2023 Edelman Trust Barometer.

The United States remains the world's richest economy and the most productive and innovative. None of its peers or competitors can keep pace. America continues to produce a quarter of the world's output, at market exchange rates, as it did in 1990, and now accounts for 58% of G7 GDP.[9] America wins because of the quality of its education, innovation, and patents; its talent attraction; the increased number of workers; the quality of its companies; the tax system; and (since the Obama health care reforms) a more generous welfare system. This is true not only for the wealthiest, but also for the middle class, though inequalities worryingly increase and the access to the American Dream appears increasingly to be the preserve of the most privileged. Despite this overall success, corporate leaders in the U.S. are concerned about a dysfunctional government, a polarized media, and a far from united population. Because of its industrial economic success, the U.S. will need to re-skill its workforce as disruptive technologies like AI take hold, inevitably destroying some jobs while creating new ones with higher value-added and barriers to entry. Policymakers will be called upon not only to finance these transitions – as they did recently with the Inflation Reduction Act – but to do so with a new vision. The societal context has indeed changed, and the state must regain its essential traits. A new partnership with the business world is now needed.

The constitution of Europe has been a dream and a passion of generations since Winston Churchill's post-World War II wish for a "kind of United States of Europe." Its record is mixed, and it has sometimes disappointed its citizens. Brexit did not help. Still, the fact that the continent's 500 million inhabitants are proud to call themselves Europeans can only be positive in the context of Europe's history, and the complexities even within the borders of its nation-state members.

In addition, there is an emerging belief in the creation of enterprises of scale and scope capable of competing on an equal footing with the U.S. and China. Henry Kissinger's evergreen joke, "Give me Europe's phone number", his wry comment on the lack of centralized European decision-making, may finally be outdated. Today, Airbus, Europe's largest aerospace company with more than 130,000 employees, is perhaps the only example of Europe creating a player that can compete with its

---

[9] *The Economist*, April 13, 2023.

American archrival, Boeing. Airbus is at the forefront of the aviation industry, building the most innovative commercial aircraft and consistently winning about half of all commercial aircraft orders.[10] The corporation delivers an average of 600 commercial aircraft per year, generating revenues of €52.1 billion (about $55 billion).

In the air, Europe competes with the United States in terms of size, but it lags in other industries. As of June 2023, the largest EU company by market capitalization was the French luxury goods conglomerate LVMH, with approximately $460 billion, ranking it 13th in the world.

But other industries make a difference in terms of geopolitical power and cutting-edge expertise: defense, pharmaceuticals, financial services, digital, software, energy, electronics, to name a few. These industries are leaders in innovation, in part because of the prolific startup world that populates their respective value chains.

In terms of market capitalization, there is now a clear gap between the United States and the European Union. The latter is still focused on domestic champions, as opposed to world leaders. The same conclusion applies when comparing European companies with China.

In the strategic software industry, German-based SAP was ranked 71st in the world and 7th in its industry in June 2023, with a market capitalization of $134 billion. US-based Oracle and Salesforce had market capitalizations of $300 billion and $220 billion, respectively. There is no European financial institution in the top 100. As of June 2023, BNP Paribas has a market capitalization of $73.74 billion, making it the 195th most valuable company in the world. By comparison, JPMorgan Chase has a market capitalization of $405.7 billion in June 2023, which means it is number 19 in the same ranking. Apple, Amazon, Microsoft, Alphabet, and Tesla – all U.S. companies – have market caps above $1 trillion. As noted above, it was Europe that established the global mobile standard: GSM. In the United States, however, 320 million Americans enjoy the services of three nationwide wireless providers – Verizon, AT&T, and T-Mobile. In Europe, there are at least three or four telecom operators per member state. This is a key example of a situation where the lack of policy primacy means that stakeholders are fragmented and correspondingly less prosperous.

---

[10] Source: Airbus website.

European corporate leaders therefore have a historic opportunity to lead. French President Emmanuel Macron initiated such a discussion in 2019 with the idea of a common defense system, which has so far fallen on deaf ears. However, circumstances have prepared potentially more fertile ground. The European Next Generation EU (NGEU) fund, the European-led version of the Marshall Plan, financed by the current partial mutualization of the common debt, could lead to a grand vision, a vision in which companies can participate and contribute, since it will require the capabilities of each company. Enhanced capabilities in competition will in turn better serve all stakeholders.

Last but not least is a strong academic community. That the four pillars of the democratic system are structurally out of sync can no longer be ignored, and academia can be instrumental in recalibrating them. Many laudable practices, such as sustainability, have already found their way into university curricula. As we prepare future generations to lead a world of rapidly evolving complexity, academia can prepare future generations to be fully aware of the needs of society and fully competent to ensure a stable and prosperous society for all.

6.6   Summary

We are targeting the democracies of Europe and North America, and those around the world who share their values. The challenges are daunting, as these countries' populations age and an unprecedented mass of immigrants knocks on their doors. At the same time, these countries face economic and social challenges at home: social justice, inclusion, unemployment, strained welfare systems, upskilling of the workforce, and the like.

Governments need to be more competent to adequately deliver on the promise and obligation of the primacy of politics. Corporations can help spread a better understating of the issues and transfer know-how. The media would also benefit from a different corporate attitude that, while staying out of the political arena, improves its positioning for the benefit of policymakers and stakeholders. Over time, this renewed collaboration will need to find creative ways to help and support elected officials.

Critically for the beleaguered CEO, the IRG helps top management fully explain its strategic plan: its implications, its benefits, and the necessary trade-offs. This proactive leadership will help avoid misunderstandings and anticipate adverse reactions that can be caused by a lack of knowledge or, worse, by manipulation and ideology. Public expectations must be carefully managed to avoid messianic demands that no company can realistically meet. Today's world is one of double-edged opportunities. This book has highlighted some of the challenges that remain for policymakers – officials elected to mediate between the strength of capital (and the profits that must be returned to investors) and the general welfare of the population. For too long, this intermediary role has been poorly performed, so companies now need to share their expertise to help policymakers understand the scale, dynamics, and consequences of choices – and, where necessary, to help implement those choices.

The war in Ukraine shocked the West into temporary cohesion. The pandemic has also highlighted the need for strong, transformative public institutions and governments. But this may simply be a rehearsal. The other challenges ahead will require just as much, if not more. In this scenario, the IRG applies realism to support a thorough and seamlessly managed corporate realignment by adapting operating models that may unwittingly be nearing obsolescence in this rapidly evolving situation. The IRG provides a comprehensive system for measuring, managing, and shaping public expectations, an engagement that benefits both the company and the public. What's more, the IRG allows companies to embrace change, fill the evolutionary void, and help policymakers make the necessary changes.

Among the dangers ahead, populism is attracting more and more people and has shown its dangers. It is important that this not also be a rehearsal. At the same time, executives are not politicians and are under constant pressure to focus on their core business. An important part of the IRG's function is to absorb much of the workload of expected and even required corporate action in its wider environment in the near future. Here we refer to a new set of expectations that is insistently making its way to the desk of the corporate executive. Far from gesture politics, it is becoming a corporate imperative as fundamental to reputation as it is to the bottom line. Whether welcomed or seen as a burden, companies should seek to influence through action, ensuring that it is relevant, effective, and focused. Also essential is proactive, competent, and authoritative leadership, looking to where corporate growth and prosperity can be generated in the process.

Afterword
by *KC Sullivan*

At CNBC our reporting and executive interviews provide us with a prime view of how corporations are operating in the dynamic and changing global environment. Not too long ago publicly traded companies focused on their balance sheet, share price, and regulatory policy, but today companies find the need to address many public concerns, as well.

Author Fernando Napolitano observes that there is an erosion of trust in many of our pillars of influence including governments and news media around the world. He points out that the polarization of political systems has impacted the ability of governments to effectively address issues important to life in democracies; and how societal polarization is impacting news media's ability to deliver the facts when facts themselves are constantly in question.

As a result, a vacuum around both policy making and arbiters of trusted information has emerged. The public, customers and employees are more conscious of and demanding of the role a corporation and its CEO play in society. Thus, corporate leaders are finding it necessary to think of different stakeholders in addition to their consumers, investors, and their workforce and to provide a sense of stability and predictability, allowing business to flourish.

And as the role of the corporation in society has increased, the public contemplation and addressing of social issues has become an expected duty of today's CEOs.

The problem that follows this increased involvement in social issues, is that many of the stances taken are often not tied to a company's focus, and thus, increasingly putting corporations in the cross hairs of public opinion and politicians, which can undermine its mission and often hampering the business itself.

Mr. Napolitano makes a strong case for a data led process that assesses a company's effectiveness. Mr. Napolitano has established the Influence Relevance and Growth (IRG) system, a solution-oriented approach worthwhile pursuing for global leaders trying to navigate these exact challenges. For the news media, IRG might provide an interesting platform for discussion by shareholders, politicians, consumers and employees around the involvement of corporations in society.

The IRG proposes an innovative, data led methodology that aims to be politically neutral, and fact based, which can be particularly helpful as the role of the CEO has been politically charged by all sides. Grounding an assessment of a company's efforts in data allows for a fairer and more unbiased look of a company's effectiveness.

By taking a holistic view and approach that embraces the modern societal environment, the IRG methodology is a tool that today's corporate leaders could certainly use to help balance business value with good corporate citizenship.

Authors

Fernando Napolitano
President & CEO NEWEST

Fernando joined Booz Allen Hamilton in 1990 becoming Senior Vice President, Italy's managing director and member of the European management team. He specialized in telecom and energy industries. He served as an independent member of the board of directors of Enel S.p.A., Mediaset S.p.A., CIRA (Italian Aerospace Research Center), AMRI, Albany, New York. Previously he worked for Procter & Gamble Marketing division in Rome and Laben, a Leonardo company.
He graduated with honors in Economy from Federico II University in Naples, Italy, and in 1984 was European Champion U.21 with the Italian National Water polo team. Subsequently graduated MSM from Brooklyn Poly (now NYU) and AMP from Harvard Business School.

Stefano Caselli
Dean, SDA Bocconi School of Management

Stefano Caselli is the Dean of SDA Bocconi School of Management and he is Full Professor of Banking & Finance at the Department of Finance and Algebris Chair in "Long-Term Investment and Absolute Return" at Bocconi University.

KC Sullivan
President, CNBC

KC Sullivan is President of CNBC, the recognized world leader in business news. He is responsible for the network's TV and Digital news operations, original primetime programming and subscription products. A thirteen-year veteran of NBCUniversal, Sullivan has spent more than a decade in leadership roles across the company's portfolio in both the U.S. and overseas.